FROM CALVINIST TO CATHOLIC

PETER KREEFT

From Calvinist
to Catholic

IGNATIUS PRESS   SAN FRANCISCO

Cover art:
Top: Portrait of John Calvin by François Stuerhelt, c. 1602–1652. Engraving, from the collection of the Rijksmuseum. Public domain.

Bottom: Statue of Saint Peter, Vatican City. Photo by iam_os on Unsplash.com

Cover design by John Herreid

© 2025 by Ignatius Press, San Francisco
All rights reserved
ISBN 978-1-62164-696-9 (HB)
ISBN 978-1-64229-307-4 (eBook)
Library of Congress Control Number 2024950416
Printed in the United States of America ∞

CONTENTS

INTRODUCTION

The three best things I ever did in my life were (1) to become a Catholic, (2) to marry my wife, and (3) to have kids. This book is about the first thing. All my other work—my so-called teaching "career" and my writing "career" (over one hundred books so far)—is trivial compared to any one of those three gigantic things.

I put the word "career" in quotation marks deliberately. For Socrates, the archetype and spiritual grandfather of all philosophers, teaching was not a "career". Like Jesus and Buddha, he never took money for his teaching and would regard today's "professors" of philosophy as intellectual prostitutes. Like Jesus and Buddha, he would never get tenure at any university today because he wrote no books or articles at all. Yet he was the second greatest teacher in history.

I've had three truly great "role models" as philosophy teachers: William Harry Jellema at Calvin, Brand Blanshard at Yale, and Father Norris Clarke at Fordham. Jellema was a Calvinist, Blanshard was an atheist, and Clarke was a Catholic and a priest. But my wife, my children, and my Church were my three best teachers. Marriage is a profound teacher, and in the Catholic mind-set, marriage is so necessary that even celibate nuns, priests, and monks marry: they marry the Church. Kids are also effective teachers; in fact, having kids matures parents just as much as having parents matures kids.

But this book is about only one of those three teachers, the Church, and my road to Rome and home. So it's not a complete personal autobiography, any more than is C. S. Lewis' (*Surprised by Joy*). Comparing my book with Lewis' is like comparing Little League with Major League baseball, but that's the *kind* of story this is: its center is meant to be, not the traveler, but the road.

Lewis said, in his preface to *Surprised by Joy*, that he found the writing of his own autobiography to be "suffocatingly subjective"—even though it was focused on "joy" itself rather than on Lewis. I, too, find the enterprise of autobiography "suffocatingly subjective". I nominate

Facebook for an award for being the most insufferably egotistical enter-prise and the biggest waste of time in human history.

I wrote this book only because Mark Brumley, my Ignatius Press editor, never stopped politely badgering me to write it. Even now I'm not certain it is not a mistake. It's a kind of mirror, and I think there are no mirrors in Heaven. My story *has* to be about me, of course, but I want it to be above all a story about God and His grace in my life. I am the author of this book, but God is the Author of the author. Unfortunately, I do not have the God's-eye point of view I would like to have, but I can at least aspire to get a little closer to that point of view than to the subjectivism I like to call "ingrown eyeballs", which are as delightful as ingrown toenails. I think "suf-focatingly subjective" is a pretty accurate description of the psy-chology of Hell, and of both the pride and despair that lead there, just as "joyfully self-forgetful" is a pretty accurate description of the psychology of Heaven and of the saints.

"All roads lead to Rome" in the sense that the destination (the objective truth of the Catholic Faith) is one even though the sub-jective, personal paths to that destination are many. There can be only one objectively true road map, but there are many subjective, personal journeys. Each journey is unique because each person is unique; that's why totalitarianism never lasts, no matter how efficient it is. And no matter how familiar the essential themes of the conver-sion story may be, the details are always different; and, as they say, "God is in the details."

It's also said that "the Devil is in the details." A road always runs in two directions, and we meet many traveling in both directions. Our greatest Friend, who is Truth (Logos) Incarnate, and our greatest Enemy, who is the Father of Lies, have both erected signs along the road, and discernment and discrimination are essential.

I do not believe all who call themselves Catholics go to Heaven or that all who do not, do not; for the Catholic Church herself teaches the opposite. God is infinite in mercy, very tricky, and provides many backdoor entrances to His commodious Heavenly mansion in addi-tion to the Church, which is His visible front door.

Along this road to Rome, if you join me on my journey, you will find both particulars and universals: both particular people, places, and events and also timeless and universal issues and arguments about saints, sinners, scandals, sacraments, salvation, and systems of philosophy and theology; about history and mystery, music, miracles, mysticism, missions, and Mary, mingled with mercifully minimal mishmash about me.

My title is a bit misleading because Calvin and Calvinism have never had the crucial centrality in my life that Catholicism has had. I was a Christian first, an Evangelical second, a Protestant third, and a Calvinist fourth; and most Calvinists I know would agree with that hierarchy. But some readers will be interested in the exotic creature called the Calvinist, so I will describe that creature as I knew him, both in others and in myself when I was one of them for twenty-one years.

My religion was always central to my life, but I was never a "religious fanatic" like my high school ex-girlfriend's new boyfriend, who literally would not date, kiss, or even hold hands with her until they had prayed together. Calvinists are not usually *that* "religious", but they do usually take both their personal religiosity and their common theology very seriously; and they tend to have more serious and thoughtful objections to Catholicism than most other non-Catholics do. The operative objections to Catholicism that are most common in our culture today almost always center, not on God, but on the Church's philosophy of sex, which they almost infallibly misunderstand, unless they've studied Pope Saint John Paul II's "Theology of the Body".

This book is really three books. Chapters 1–10 are a pre-conversion autobiography. Chapters 11–22 are the theological issues and reasons that led me to Rome. Chapters 23–32 are a post-conversion autobiography.

I

Choices

Our lives are determined by choices, because life is a series of roads, and roads fork into two or more, and the choice of one fork must always be made at the expense of the other forks of "the road not taken" (Robert Frost). Many of the choices that determine the journey of our lives are made, not *by* us, but *for* us—not only by the other *people* in our lives but also by both the remote and immediate past, by the evolution of the universe and the human species, by the whole history of mankind on this planet, and by our ancestors, our extended family into the past.

All our lives are stories. That is why storytelling, or narrative, is the most fundamental and universal of all human arts. And since a story requires a storyteller, our story is evidence for a Divine Providence. For if not, then our art of storytelling is inherently deceptive, for it is our imposition of design and order, our illusion of free choice and meaning on an objective reality that is formless, random, *logos*-less, void of order and meaning and design, "full of sound and fury, *signifying* nothing", in the words of Macbeth, who is on his way to damnation. That is why no determinist (like B. F. Skinner) can write good novels. (His *Walden Two* is boring and ridiculous.)

My favorite example of this divine design in my ancestry is the acorn that fell from a tree one day in a city park over a hundred years ago where my great-grandfather sat alone on a bench eating his lunch. The acorn hit a branch and bounced. Had it bounced to the left rather than to the right, it would have hit a soggy, grassy patch of ground and made no noise. Instead, it bounced to the right and landed on a pile of dry autumn leaves, making a sharp sound that called my great-grandfather's attention to it. He turned his head in that direction and thus "happened" to notice, just behind that pile of leaves, a pretty girl sitting alone on another park bench. Overcoming his shyness, he chose to sashay over to her, pretending nonchalance, and politely asked her whether she would like some company or an extra apple from his lunchbox. She, too, chose to overcome her shyness and accepted both his company and his apple. A fruitful conversation ensued. He asked and received her permission for a date, and a year later he was asking her father's permission for her hand in marriage. If that acorn had dropped one inch to the left rather than to the right, I and all my family would not have come into existence.

That story is invented, but it is totally realistic. That is how things in real life do actually happen. As Pascal notes, if Cleopatra's nose had been a quarter of an inch longer, the whole history of the world would have been changed. If that one particular sperm had not gotten into your mother's ovum before the other twenty million passengers arrived at that taxi stop, you would have been a very different person.

In his Pulitzer Prize-winning little masterpiece *The Bridge of San Luis Rey*, Thornton Wilder wrote, concerning the apparently random story of human life, with all its inexplicable tragedies, "Some say that to the gods we are like flies swatted idly by boys on a summer day. Others say that not a hair falls from our head without the will of the Heavenly Father." It's either all or nothing, God or nothing; all design or no design.

Divine Providence and human free choices, divine purposes and human purposes, not only do not contradict each other but imply each other. Both are necessary if human life is a story, a drama, rather than a random, pointless brute fact; that is, if there are such things as persons, entities with intelligence and free choice, real characters, interacting in a real story whose meaning they do not merely invent but discover. Every story ever told reconciles human free will and divine design, predestination, or destiny. There is no story if the characters are only predictable machines, and there is no story if there is no storyteller, no script, all ad lib.

The fact that you, a person with free will, have freely made the meaningful choice to read this book, this story, a story about another person who has also freely made meaningful and important choices in his life, is a very strong reason for believing in both free will and the existence of God. If there is design, there must be a Designer. If there is a play, there must be a Playwright. If life is a story, there must be a Storyteller.

There are other reasons for believing in the existence of God, the Divine Designer; but the fact that human life is a story is one of the best ones. There are other reasons for believing in free will (for instance, if we are not free, then all morality and all justice is meaningless; we do not praise or blame, reward or punish, preach to or plead with, machines), but the fact that human life is a story is one of the best ones.

ﱲ ﱲ ﱲ

Here are the ten choices in my life that seem to me to have been the most momentous and life-changing. I say "seem to me" in order to leave room deliberately for the very likely possibility that from God's point of view I have inadvertently omitted some of the most important choices of all. For since none of the characters in our play are identical with the Playwright, our point of view is not identical with His point of view. (Surprise, surprise!)

1. My choice, as a teenager, to ask my wise Calvinist pastor, Rev. Theodore Jansma, some questions about a fascinating book I had read by Dorothy Sayers (*Creed or Chaos?*). Recognizing a budding philosopher, he recommended that I also read Dorothy's friend C. S. Lewis, who has come to shape my mind more than any other author.

2. My choice to attend Eastern Christian High School rather than the public high school in Paterson, New Jersey, where I received my first and most foundational education in Christian thinking.

3. My choice to go to Calvin College, where this Christian thinking was taken up to the next level, which in fact turned out to be the Catholic level, since I saw Catholicism as the logical conclusion of the fundamental Christian and biblical principles I had already accepted as what C. S. Lewis calls "Mere Christianity". (See the last chapter in my *Handbook of Catholic Apologetics* for a summary of this argument: that every distinctively Catholic doctrine is the consummation and perfection of a doctrine shared by Protestants as well as Catholics. I am more Evangelical now as a Catholic than I ever was as an Evangelical Protestant, just as most Jews who become Christians say they are now more Jewish, not less, since Christianity is the fulfillment and consummation of Judaism, not its replacement.)

4. My choice to give my life to Christ by enrolling in a preseminary curriculum at Calvin College to train to become a pastor.

5. My choice to become an English major instead because I knew I was much better at reading and writing than at pastoring. (One is always better at what one loves more deeply and instinctively.) Pastoring is more important than reading and writing because people are more important than words, but that does not mean that all should become pastors. "Pastors" means "shepherds"; and like most "intellectuals", I subconsciously succumbed to an instinctive snobbery about ordinary people's resemblance to sheep. I still hate "small talk", but I now see that as a fault, not a virtue.

6. My choice to become a philosophy major, for the same reason: I loved it, and I was good at it.

7. My choice to *investigate* Catholicism with an open mind, long before I realized that there was a live animal behind that door that I chose to open and peek through.

8. My choice to believe Catholicism for the only honest reason one should ever believe anything: because it is true; and thus to accept Baptism into it. (It was "conditional re-baptism", not because the Church claimed to know that Protestant baptism was invalid, but because she did *not* know. That's based on the same principle that rationally justifies being anti-abortion: not because we know with certainty that a human fetus is a fetal human, a human person, but because we can't know that it isn't.)

9. My choice to marry, and to marry this particular person, because of who she was, and to have children, although we did not know who they would be.

10. My ongoing, unspectacular, ordinary, and undramatic choice to be faithful to all these choices—which is the most important choice of all. Kierkegaard says that a "knight of faith" conquers the most formidable dragon of all: time and change.

2

Ancestry

I was born (How original! Has there ever been an autobiography from someone who was *not* born?) in 1937, toward the end of the Great Depression, in Paterson, New Jersey, a once-prosperous mill town of about 135,000 that has turned into a seedy semi-slum. William Carlos Williams won a Pulitzer Prize for his epic poem "Paterson", which he used as a symbol of America's twentieth-century decadence. Larry Doby, Lou Costello, and Father George Rutler were also born in Paterson.

Most of the Dutch immigrants to America around the turn of the (twentieth) century landed in either Paterson, New Jersey, Grand Rapids, Michigan, or Pella, Iowa. There is a story that explains why some of them founded Amsterdam, New York, which is about two hundred miles north of New York City. It is that the first Dutch immigrants settled on Amsterdam Avenue in northern Manhattan, and they invited the second wave of immigrants to join them there. Their directions were vague: just walk north from Ellis Island until you get to Amsterdam Avenue. The second wave of immigrants missed Amsterdam Avenue, and, being Dutch, were very stubborn, so they just kept walking north for two hundred miles before they came to the conclusion that they must have missed it, so they called the town they founded there, just north of Albany, "Amsterdam".

Paterson is part of "The Sopranos" state. One of my favorite lines is from a Woody Allen movie in which he and Diane Keaton are having a picnic outdoors on a beautiful day. Diane asks him, "Should we say grace before we eat? What religion are you?" And Woody replies, "I'm an atheist, thank God. But on a beautiful day like this I could bring myself to believe that there exists an omnipresent divine mind pervading all parts of the universe—except, of course, certain areas of northern New Jersey."

My mother's parents, Peter and Mattie Comtabad, lived in the top half of a narrow little two-family house in Paterson, on Hopper Street, on the border with Prospect Park. Their (and, later, our) large, plain church (the Sixth Reformed) was one block away. They had no car, no garage, no driveway, a three-foot-wide alley on each side of the house, and no central heating. The house was heated by a large coal stove in the kitchen. It slept seven people—Peter, Mattie, Peter Junior ("June"), Adrian, Ada, Lucy, and Lena—in five rooms and an attic. There was a kitchen, two small bedrooms, one bathroom, and a large dining room and living room, which, being unheated, were seldom occupied except for formal family dinners, visits, and conversations. Formality was more important than comfort. My mother and her two sisters slept in the unheated attic under layers of homemade quilts next to wrapped hot bricks in the winter. There were also screened porches, front and back, which became warm greenhouses in winter when windows replaced the screens. The first floor, identical to the second, was occupied by Adrian, the oldest boy, and Sadie, his wife, when they got married.

My grandfather had a rusty old lawnmower (it made a sound like a cat), even though his lawn was only about forty square feet. The backyard was a large vegetable garden and a chicken coop. He was a bricklayer, walked a mile to and from work six days a week, and had bleeding hands every winter. He retired in his nineties. He literally saved his pennies. One penny a day for nearly a lifetime paid for his generous gift to me and my wife of a cemetery burial plot. (I'm told that the traditional Irish marriage proposal is: "How'd ye like to be buried with my folk?")

His generosity was built on "pinchpenny" Republican economics. The one thing I remember him saying to me most often, like a mantra, was: "Save your money." The kitchen table, the center of the house's activity, was always covered by *two* tablecovers of durable oilcloth, and when we ate there, he put newspapers over the top layer for additional protection. There was a radio in the kitchen that I never remember being turned on. The living room was for living (conversation and company), and the dining room was for dining. But it was used for Easter, Christmas, and Thanksgiving only.

There was, of course, no TV and no refrigerator: the iceman came round regularly for the icebox. The cellar had no washing machine (only a sink and scrubbing board). There was electricity, but lights were shut off with religious care when leaving the room, to save pennies.

Grandpa Comtabad was short, skinny, and wiry, and his wife, Mattie, was enormously fat. He was the sovereign lord and master of the family, and Mattie was the peacemaker. I do not remember him ever smiling. His wife supplied all the smiles in the family. If they had been one person instead of two, they would have been admirably complete.

All four of my grandparents were immigrants from the Netherlands. Uneducated, they all learned English quickly. My father's family (the Kreefts) were very poor and very close, probably because of the poverty. My mother's family (the Comtabads) was a little less poor and a lot less close. I think the children were impatient to leave the house they grew up in. I sensed a kind of brittleness or even fear in most of the Comtabads, and I suspect that my mother's extreme personal conservatism and aversion to change and adventure were due to her father's rather tyrannical personality. I'm told that when he learned that his son Adrian, as a teenager, had asked a Catholic girl for a date, he threw him down the stairs, breaking some of his bones.

My father's father died when he was twelve, and his mother (Jennie Kreeft) held the family together by working every day cleaning houses and doing sewing, while three of her four children went to full-time work after eighth grade. My father, the smartest one, was the only one who finished high school. Aunt Edna never married, Aunt Chrissie in her forties married a man in his fifties, and Uncle Jack married in his fifties. I was the only grandchild.

My father told me that he had to fight with his mother for a long time for permission to leave the house and get married. Grandma Kreeft was hard and tough and strong, and in constant pain from arthritis all the time I knew her. Her children grew up poor and uneducated but not repressed, nasty-minded, stupid, or unhappy. I never saw any backbiting, disrespect, or lack of love from any of them to me or to each other. Their loyalty to their family and their faith were fierce and happy. They were able to enjoy life despite their poverty (or perhaps even because of it, if we believe the Sermon on the Mount).

My father told me that he remembers having fish or meat once a week (usually hamburger or sausage). Their staple was hutspot, which was a big bowl of mashed potatoes, with meat gravy but no meat, and numerous vegetables from their backyard garden. Another was pea soup, with a large ham bone and hard, stale bread. Eggs were plentiful because they had chickens. When a chicken grew beyond egg-laying age, the family had the treat of chicken meat.

In my experience, the food of the poor typically tastes better than the food of the rich. The tastiest food I ever had was from the Benedictine monks in the Mojave Desert at Valyermo, California, that they said cost them ninety-nine cents for three meals a day. (This was in 1964.) Like my grandparents, the monks had plenty of chickens (also pigs and sheep), grew all their fruits and vegetables fresh, and made their own bread, jam, and sauces.

When I was a kid, I remember postage stamps costing three cents, newspapers two cents, and ice cream cones five cents. My first full-time summer job, at my father's factory in 1954, paid $42.50 a week. During the postwar "gasoline wars", gasoline cost sixteen cents a gallon. During the war, when gasoline was rationed, my father rode a bike to and from work five miles away. When I inherited the bike, I loved it like a friend. It was made of heavy, black, unpainted metal. It was thin and stripped: no fenders, hand brakes, basket, gears, or gear shift. Its apparently immortal life ended when I and it together crashed into a suddenly opening parked car door on my way to high school on a foggy, rainy day. I was proud of its power: it took the car door off one of its hinges. Lots of blood, quick trip to hospital, no broken bones or organs.

My father's family lived in a similar house to my mother's, larger but with the exact same room layout; but they had a driveway and, after the war, a car. It was in Prospect Park, eight blocks from the border with Paterson, higher up the hill of Haledon Avenue, with a great view of New York City, eighteen miles away, from the second-story porch. My father and his brother slept in the unheated attic. (I wonder why the Comtabads put the girls in the unheated attic, while the Kreefts put the boys there.) My father once was made to spend the night in the chicken coop in the backyard as punishment for some prank. When his father came to end the prison sentence in the morning and asked, "How are you?" my father answered, "Great. That was fun. Can I sleep here tonight, too?"

After graduating from high school, my father took evening courses at Pratt Institute of Industrial Design in Brooklyn (you could get everywhere cheaply by train in those days) and worked his way up though the ranks from errand boy to Chief Engineer at Morrison Machine Company. The factory was four blocks long and employed about one thousand people. He tried to interest me in the engineering problems he had solved each working day, to little avail. I remember my great relief when he told me, "I love my work, but you don't have to. You can choose your own career; it doesn't have to be like mine."

In his eighties, he was still learning: to read the New Testament in the original, he taught himself Greek. His mechanical abilities skipped a generation to take root again in my daughter, who also took courses at Pratt, taught both science and art, and designed museum exhibits for children. In contrast to both, I am clumsy with tools and technology and at home in words rather than numbers. On the verbal part of my SATs and GREs, I scored 100% (which was an 800 at the time) but only a 550 (barely passing) on the mathematical. To remember phone numbers, I have to change them to letters; even when they make no sense, I remember how they sound. When I play chess, I rarely calculate more than one or two moves ahead, yet my intuitive sense sometimes wins games against superior players.

My family went to church every Sunday morning and evening, and my father went a third time on Sunday afternoons for worship in Dutch, as well as to a "prayer meeting" every Wednesday evening. Sunday church attendance was not mandatory but voluntary, and it was nearly 100 percent. Contrast today's Catholics in America, 80 percent of whom don't go at all even though it *is* mandatory.

We had a prayer and Bible reading before every meal. I was not particularly pious, but I took this as normal, though I never felt "natural" about non-liturgical, personal prayers in public. I found "Sunday school" a bit boring and confusing but not oppressive. The teachers were all sincere, unselfish, and happy, and I imbibed what was in their faces more than what was in their words. And I learned the Bible very, very well.

As a pre-teen, I was not embarrassed by their religiosity either at home or in church because it seemed not only sincere but natural, reasonable, and human. The one exception was their long personal extemporaneous prayers, both at home (meals) and in church (the pastor's "long prayer" was part of our "liturgy"). I instinctively sensed the truth that deep, high, holy, hard, and beautiful things need formality and liturgy, not only informality and extemporaneousness. I have always felt the rightness of the distinction between public and private, collective and individual, liturgical and personal, objective and subjective, truth and love; and I felt the wrongness of the confusion or blending of the two: both the public "sharing" of private feelings and loves and also the personalizing and subjectivizing of objective truths, goods, and beauties. Both were holy, but in different ways, like men and women, justice and mercy, dogs and cats, white and black. How could anyone love gray?

Sex was not a topic of polite conversation among us Dutch Calvinists. It was neither discouraged and suppressed nor explained and glorified. And like everything else, it was put into the larger context of religious "piety", the word that used to mean both respect for family and ancestors and respect for God or the gods. It was holy, i.e., "set-apart", not to be handled casually or at will.

However, it was naturally the butt of jokes, the most famous being: Why are Calvinists forbidden to have sex standing up? Because it might lead to dancing. (Dancing, card playing, and moviegoing were the three "worldly" sins we had been warned against. Divorce, drinking, and Democrats gradually replaced them.)

Ironically, of the approximately fifty Protestant families I knew as a child, not one of them contained a divorcée. Out of the approximately fifty Catholic families I know today, not one of them does not. I judge The Pill, and the Sexual Revolution that it made possible, to have been the single most radical and personal revolution, in both behavior and thought, in all of modern history, and the main entrance into the Brave New World. If you want to see our future, read that prophetic book.

3

Childhood

I was an only child but not a lonely child. My parents and I lived in Haledon, a lower-middle-class suburb of about ten thousand, one mile west of the city of Paterson. Between Haledon and Paterson was Prospect Park, a single square mile whose population then was nearly 100 percent Dutch Calvinist and now has become mostly Muslim. America has been formed by waves of immigrants each climbing a step up the social ladder to occupy places that the last wave of immigrants left for higher climbing. Nearly everyone I knew, like myself, had parents or grandparents who were born in Holland, and they were all members of either the Reformed Church in America (RCA), as we were, or the breakaway Christian Reformed Church (CRC), which ran Calvin College in Grand Rapids, Michigan. I don't know what issue caused the breakaway, but even then half the RCA was "modernist" and half was not.

My parents, when they married, had moved from downtown Paterson, with its large businesses, factories, apartment houses, and department stores, to Haledon, with its one- and two-story homes, small businesses, and mom and pop stores. In one direction (west) only a few blocks away were woods, steep hills, streams, and a large quarry. Within two blocks of my house there was a diner, two gas stations, a small factory, a butcher shop, a barber, a bakery, a flower shop, a fruit store, my elementary school, and the "candy store", which must have been bigger on the inside than on the outside, for it contained everything a kid could desire: ice cream, soda, an amazingly large assortment of candy, comic books, local and distant newspapers, some in foreign languages, magazines, including six monthly science fiction magazines, small toys, party stuff, school supplies, some basic groceries, and cheap gifts. The first supermarket came right after the war.

In my senior year in high school, my family and I moved to Wyckoff, the next step up the ladder, a tony, leafy suburb designed for cars,
not walking. The nearest store was half a mile away. Our two-story
two-family house in Haledon had been the biggest one on the street;
our new house in Wyckoff, a two-bedroom ranch house, was the
smallest. The house across the street looked almost exactly like Tony
Soprano's house.

While living in Haledon, we made frequent tourist trips to New
York City, only eighteen miles away. I've always seen it as the most
interesting city in the world. We were New York Giants baseball
fans, and we frequented the strangest stadium in baseball, the Polo
Grounds, where pop fly home runs to the right field foul line traveled
only 251 feet from home plate, while one to straightaway center field
went 483. I think no one ever reached that mark. Johnny Mize, our
giant-sized first baseman, hit fifty-one home runs one year, most of
them pop flies to the right. When the Giants left for San Francisco, I
became a Red Sox fan. I had a T-shirt that said "I love New York"
on one side and "I Hate the Yankees" on the other side. It confused
people. That made me happy. I was a (gentle) troublemaker. I still
am. Socrates was always my favorite philosopher.

Willie Mays was my favorite baseball player. I do not remember
a single example of racism in my family, except in friendly jokes. I
never heard the N-word except in jokes that seemed more friendly
than nasty. Anti-Semitism was much deeper and more common than
anti-Black racism. I think the reason was not primarily theological or
biological but economic. A more radical racism was present during
the war: the Japanese were dehumanized as "Japs", yet the Germans,
while feared, were not dehumanized as "Krauts", probably because
the Dutch are so close to them that they were labeled "plat-Deutsch",
or "low German".

I vividly remember my parents' shock when Hitler conquered
Holland in a few days. They knew of Hitler's raging hatred for the
Jews (although they did not know the full horrors of the Holocaust
yet) and did not share it. After all, our Lord was Jewish, both in blood
and in belief.

Most families I knew lived in Prospect Park, three blocks away, in
two-family houses. A family typically lived in one flat and rented out
the other one until the first of their children got married and inherited it. The Dutch are typically very practical and frugal.

Everyone I knew was Dutch, frugal, conservative, and Republican. We saw Democrats as financially irresponsible, naïve, and halfway to Socialism, which was halfway to Communism.

My first love, at a great distance, was Doris, in fourth grade. She looked like an Italian Barbie. Her eyes were large and round, and her long black hair shimmered and shook. In high school, I had one date with another Doris, a preacher's daughter, who was blonde and beautiful and icily polite. Also in high school, I persuaded the prettiest girl in school, Judy, she of the ready smile and the cute nose, to "go steady" with me. But my fascination was only with her face, not with her mind. Also, she politely resisted even my mildly erotic advances. (Almost everyone was *polite* in those far distant days.) When I went to college, as she did not, I decided she was "nice but boring", somewhat like my mother. (Sorry, Mom, I really did love you, and I know you loved me. But I didn't want to marry your clone.) In college, for a short time I dated Virginia, the homecoming queen and a dead ringer for Elizabeth Taylor, until I finally discovered the obscure and mysterious truth that minds were as important as bodies and that hers was simply mixed up, far away, and unapproachable. (That discovery took a long time because all males whose veins run with blood rather than water are genetically predestined to be shallow, defenseless suckers for female beauty.) Finally, after college, I found Maria, a woman whose soul and mind were as beautiful as her body, and I married her. But that's another story.

Our "tribal" loyalty and provincialism (as Dutch, as Calvinists, and as Protestants) had both a good side and a bad side. For instance, we all firmly believed that the pope was the Antichrist and that the Catholic Church was the Satanic "whore of Babylon" mentioned in the Book of Revelation. My parents believed that, too, but they tempered the personal prejudice and were polite to their few Catholic acquaintances. However, their circle of friends and family included no non-Calvinists. It was a religious issue that was at the heart of both their anti-Catholicism and their much milder anti-Semitism, and it was "salvation by faith" versus "works-righteousness". I think they were right to focus on the most practical question of all, salvation, or how to get to Heaven, but wrong to separate simplistically its two aspects, faith and works; right to think it is ridiculous and arrogant to see ourselves as good enough to deserve Heaven by our good deeds (how many is enough?), but wrong to think that

Catholics, Jews, and Muslims were so ridiculous and arrogant as to think that.

I felt secure and basically happy throughout my childhood. I remember only three times when I felt a fear that approached terror.

One of these occasions was waking up in the middle of the night when I was about three or four to see a fire that was burning down the cow barn half a block away just across the empty field next to our house. I had never seen a fire so large and close. But the scariest thing of all was listening to the terrified wails of the burning cows that had escaped and were running across our backyard lighting up the darkness like torches. I seem to remember seeing lines of fire running along the hair on their backs, but that may be only in my imagination. Years later, I used to follow fire engines on my bike, hoping for the excitement of seeing large and terrifying fires again. I never did.

Another remembered early terror was the fever dreams I had after a tonsillectomy with ether. The walls seemed to be moving, and the wallpaper turning into thousands of beetles. It hurt to scream.

Worst of all was a nightmare of the Devil, all face, no body, with a sneering clown-grin, hovering outside my second-story bedroom window. The most terrifying thing was that he made eye contact with me, with a sneering "gotcha!" grin. I was so paralyzed that I was unable to scream and woke up in a cold sweat. I also remember a nightmare of a different demon made of sparks standing in a cold white fire in my backyard. Her (it was a "her") flames had a kind of cold energy that froze my muscles so that I could not move or turn or run away.

I was only mildly afraid of two large bullies at school who habitually picked on me and the other "nerds" (we were called "eggheads" then). That was typical of public schools then, and nothing was done about it. In the Christian high school I went to next, bullying was done only on the tag football field, where it was not terrifying and was almost encouraged.

I remember no remarkable ongoing psychological terrors in my childhood except the fear, each evening from 5 to 5:30, that my father may have died at work and would never come home again. I think that terror lasted a few months. I don't know whether I picked it up unconsciously from my mother or consciously from a story I read. It was my first coping with the existential possibility of death.

I never sensed anger in either of my parents toward each other, only mild frustrations and disagreements. Strong love and respect were clearly there, though rarely expressed physically. I was occasionally spanked, with a paddle, for the usual childish offenses, and I remember being puzzled at sensing only sadness, not anger, in the spanker, which generated a corresponding sadness rather than anger in the spankee. I think this primitive discipline did more good than harm to me: although I hated and resented it, it reinforced my sense of cosmic justice and order. My pain was mild, but my fear of "The Paddle" was not. As Aron Nimzowitsch, a great chess champion, famously wrote, "the threat is more powerful than its execution." This is true in chess, in war, in politics, and in life. The one notable exception is Hell. (If Heaven must exceed all our ordinary desires, Hell must exceed all our ordinary fears and threats.)

I felt safe both at home and outside. My mother, despite her unadventurous "safety first" conservatism, never feared for me to go anywhere my bike could take me. Our world then did not include any such species as sexual predators or mass murderers. We knew there were plenty of drunks, but we never heard of drug addicts. There were criminals, but even they seemed to know their place, and that place was not in our little middle-class suburb. Kids often fought and bloodied each other, but that was not taken seriously by most parents: it was just "boys being boys". Girls were busy being girls, which to us boys was as distant and incomprehensible as the moon. They seemed shallow and giggly to us, but almost all the girls seemed happy to know and feel "in their place". That phrase today is usually insulting; then, it was comforting. We all would have been absolutely dumbfounded then to learn that today half of all teenage girls seriously contemplate suicide.

Sex was bragged about almost always, consummated almost never. Homosexuality was there, I think, but rare and closeted. Transgenderism was a fantastic joke. Personal identity and security were not distant ideals to worry about or even to strive for, but habitually taken-for-granted realities. The roles and identities that are almost universally dismissed as naïve and simplistic stereotypes today were almost universally accepted as archetypes then. That comfortable though imperfect social edifice seemed as natural and permanent as the seasons. Its current ongoing demolition feels like an earthquake.

I loved half of my elementary school teachers and hated the other half, but it made no difference to what I learned: for both kinds of teachers, I did the work and got the rewards, or else "goofed off" and didn't. I liked the teachers who were tough but fair and clear, and I hated the ones who were vague and ambiguous even when they were easy. I wanted to know exactly where I stood and what the rules were. I've long admired both Orthodox Jews and Muslims for that. But it was probably a naïve mistake to expect that education and socialization should be as certain and timeless as religion.

One of my teachers (it was in her class that I kept getting D's in "deportment" or C's in "conduct") told me she didn't like my "attitude". I never understood what that was. Was I wearing an "attitude" as I wore a shirt? If an "attitude" is a feeling, how could I change my feeling? Was there a button on my heart's keyboard that was labeled "attitude" and that I could press when needed? How could I find that button? I thought it was *her* "attitude" that caused *my* "attitude". How could I simply stop feeling that she was a stupid jerk? How can anyone feel or not feel on command?

If life was simpler then, in the forties and fifties, it was also harder and more primitive. For many years, until after the war, we had an icebox instead of an electric refrigerator. I remember helping my mother drag very large cubes of ice on my sled in the winter or in my red wagon in the summer home from the icehouse three blocks away. We had no washing machine until I was about ten. I remember how thrilled my mother was to get one. There was no dryer; we hung out all the clothes to dry on clotheslines that my father installed. They ran about fifty feet from the second-story porch across the backyard to the big cherry tree that was my favorite retreat, my "lookout", and my climbing gym. The cherries were bitter, but I ate some anyway because they were ours.

One of my jobs was to help my father shovel coal into the red, greedy mouth of the digestive system of our cellar coal furnace and to shovel away the ashes from its excretory system underneath it. I was fascinated to see such a powerful beast as fire tamed and confined so securely in a furnace. It seemed to be both dangerous and safe at the same time: a union of dynamism and stability, danger and security, unpredictable drama and structural predictability, like the plot of a good story.

Our cellar had a large wooden door in its wall that apparently led nowhere. I once asked my father what was behind it, and he answered, "Nothing." But I interpreted that as "Nothingness" and had nightmares of being sucked into a kind of Black Hole if that door ever opened. I also dreamed of a giant dead Viking rising from his grave and coming through the door. (That was an image I put to use in my one and only novel, *An Ocean Full of Angels*. It took twenty years to finish it. *Between Heaven and Hell* took six days.)

One of my favorite places was Hayden Planetarium in New York City. I loved astronomy (other worlds!), built a small telescope from a kit (a 3.5 inch reflector, 60–125 power, equatorial mount), and made maps of what I could see on the moon. From my interest in astronomy, I "got into" science fiction and, from that, fantasy. When I was deemed old enough (twelve, I think), I was allowed to spend the night outside alone in the backyard watching the Perseid meteor shower in August. I was thrilled when President Eisenhower created NASA in 1948, and I longed to be an astronaut. Or at least a pilot. I read all the books in the series "A Yankee Flyer in the R.A.F." My son, who is a pilot, must have inherited that soul-gene. I also read all thirty Hardy Boys books, and thousands of fantasy and science fiction short stories. They were trashy. But, more importantly, they were read.

Like my father, who was too young for WWI and too old for WWII, I fell just "between the cracks" between the wars in Korea and Vietnam. I followed the news about Korea as if it were a chess game played at a safe distance, while my future wife's brother-in-law was fighting there, and a little later, her other brother-in-law had buddies die in his arms in Vietnam. Two very different "points of view" about war. But though we kids played war games, and I had a lot of toy soldiers, tanks, and planes, I was never either a militarist or a pacifist. We often played pirates and staged naval battles with toy boats in brooks and ponds. We also played a lot of marbles and invented new games with them. Later, we discovered chess. I am not a psychologist, but I strongly suspect that all our games and sports, and all our dramas and stories, are our best substitutes for physical warfare.

With my best friend, Bob, I loved to explore the extensive woods, hills, and trails about half a mile from our home and to make maps of them. Later, I came to love Aquinas for making philosophical maps of just about everything thinkable. Like him, I loved both order and mystery.

I also had a three-locomotive Lionel train layout. The order was supplied, objectively, by my invention of many different track layouts,

and the mystery was supplied, subjectively, by my delightfully imprac-
tical fascination with "choo choo trains". Perhaps it was also, unconsciously, the reconciliation of mystery and order inherent in railroad
tracks themselves: that these innocent little tracks had the power to
confine these mysterious monster locomotives predictably and safely.

We played sandlot baseball (small field, two bases, four to a team),
football (it can work with just two to a team), and basketball (ditto), but
we were not in leagues organized by adults. "Necessity is the mother
of invention", and because we were few, we had to invent our own
simpler versions of our games. We invented two forms of wall ball
and field hockey (sometimes even indoors) with Ping-Pong balls and
paddles instead of pucks and sticks. I also had a Ping-Pong table in my
basement and took pride in winning most of the time.

One of our games was "war marbles", a game where each player
simply had to shoot at, hit, and thus win the other players' marbles without leaving himself vulnerable to being hit. The larger and
more complicated the battlefield (the landscape), the better. We had
many arguments about rules and violations in our invented games,
and this was excellent preparation for legal, moral, and philosophical
reasoning later in life, and for negotiating differences without force
or violence.

There was far less organization in those days, not just in our games,
but in our lives; less control, less fussiness and worry, and more fun,
freedom, and creativity than most kids experience today, when our
play is now organized and our thought is disorganized. Our maleness
and femaleness were more distinct then than they are today, and so
were our work and our play. Our play had more freedom, and our
work and thought had more order. I think there is a connection
between those two opposites. For instance, learning to play the piano
was more work than fun, but it made possible the fun of actually
playing it. I think life is a lot like a piano. The end is play, but the
necessary means is work. That's also how love works.

My father taught me to play chess, an indirect and delightful way
of learning reasoning and order, and I mastered it well enough to
beat him soon. I was fascinated with the openings, especially eso-
teric ones, because they were mainly about structures and long-range
strategy rather than short-range tactics, and that demanded intuition
(which is fun and easy for me) more than calculation (which is not).

I typically come out of the opening with a superior position and then fail in the middle game when calculation and prediction are essential. I look at chess as something like poetry or music rather than math: a drama rather than a puzzle. The actors, after all, are persons: kings, queens, knights, bishops, and pawns (servants). And it was supposedly invented by a Hindu warlord who wanted to train his soldiers for military thinking even in their leisure time. I wrote a one-hundred-page paper on the principles and strategy of my favorite opening (the Stonewall) for my freshman high school writing course and got an A for it. In high school, I also got a fifty-five-move draw with grandmaster Sammy Reshevsky, then the American champion, when he came to play twelve of us simultaneously.

I stayed up late many nights listening to New York Giants' baseball play-by-play on the radio after my parents thought I was asleep. Baseball was another world that combined justice, order, and predictability with combat, mystery, and chance; and I learned even the obscure rules and players easily. I knew my athleticism and skills were nowhere near major-league level, so my first career ambition was to be a play-by-play announcer, and I invented a number of baseball dramas, like mini-movie scripts.

The local baseball hero among us Dutchmen was "Double No-Hit, No-Run Johnny Vandermeer", a Dutchman who had lived in Hawthorne, right next to Haledon and Prospect Park, in my father's day and who had set the one major league baseball record that is probably the least likely one ever to be equaled: he pitched two no-hitters on two consecutive days for the Cincinnati Reds.

Because of Ted Williams, the Boston Red Sox became my team when the Giants moved to San Francisco. Boston became my Mecca and my home after my marriage and after four years in Philadelphia, at Villanova. I love cities in the Northeast; they are old, dirty, dangerous, inefficient, and interesting, and made for walking rather than driving. I don't feel at home in new, clean, safe, efficient, planned, rational, open, and boring cities like Dallas, Atlanta, or Orlando.

When TV came, in the fifties, there were only three black and white channels, yet every day there was something for everyone, both kids and adults. Today there are one thousand channels and nothing worth watching outside of sports or the history and geography channels unless you have the IQ of a goldfish.

I pestered my parents for pets, but they didn't work out. We tried goldfish, a turtle, a rabbit, a dog, and a canary. None lasted. The goldfish got boring, the rabbit and the turtle both ran away (probably to act in a play, *The Hare and the Tortoise*), the dog would not be toilet-trained, and the canary strangled itself between the bars of its cage. This failure in pets made me want animals all the more, and I count among my own kids' pets twenty-four fish, eight dogs, twelve cats, thirteen guinea pigs, three parakeets, three cockatiels, two rabbits, one rat, three gerbils, three hamsters, and one hedgehog (but not all at the same time). We called our backyard the "Pet Cemetery". I believe pets are powerful teachers of responsibility and compassion, and I think they should be the default norm for every family. (There are species of short-haired cats and dogs even for people with allergies.) I believe it is very probable that animals will be in Heaven. Why not? Literally everything else will be there: resurrected bodies, a bodily world, life, flowers, angels. Why should animals alone be missing?

I've always had both a love and a fear relationship to heights. In the woods half a mile from our house, atop a hill high enough for kids to call a "mountain", there was a very deep and large quarry, and its edge fascinated and terrified me. Prospect Park was at one side of it ("the hayfields"), and North Haledon on the other. I remember one idiot, stupid, ugly, and fat, who deliberately stood on the very edge and pretended to fall, just to prove how "tough" he was and to terrify the rest of us. He accomplished only the second of those two tasks.

We gave names to everything: marbles, balls, trees, trails, body parts. To move from the poetic to the pedestrian, we also had farting contests (the all-time record was seventeen in a row), and we tried, with only marginal success, to light them with matches.

When I taught at Villanova, one of the graduate students I knew, who was even more of a prankster than I, included in his one-hundred-page Master's thesis a footnote containing a supposed "disputed question" from Thomas Aquinas entitled "De Ignatione Flatuorum". It seriously considered all four Aristotelian "causes" of this bit of advanced technology. His professor approved the thesis, either because he had a sense of humor or because his Latin was not up to translating that part of it or because he just didn't read it.

I was fascinated with moving water and delightfully terrified when in the early forties our streets were so flooded that a neighbor used a rowboat to escape his house. Boats in the streets! The world of safety and order had been turned upside down. We were one block from Molly Ann's Brook, which flowed into the deep Oldham Pond half a mile away upstream, and when the pond's dam broke, each house on our street became an island. The six-foot deep, fifty-by-fifty-foot depression next to our house became a pond. The triumph of the mysterious (water) over the safe and orderly (land) was both scary and wonderful.

About ten years later, when Hurricane Carol struck the Jersey Shore on Labor Day weekend, 1954, my parents and I were on the front porch of a seaside hotel in Ocean Grove watching monster waves escape their ocean prison, leap over the boardwalk only a hundred feet away, and invade the streets beside the hotel. We saw part of the boardwalk that we had walked on only an hour earlier collapse and be sucked out to sea, together with part of a restaurant that had perched on it. The waves were moving mountains. Mountains are supposed to stay where they are! The sight was literally unforgettable, and I've been fascinated with hurricanes and great waves ever since.

I find the thrill of surfing "overhead" waves in the feeling of being one with an enormous, sublime, and terrible *power*, like a 4-6-6-4 steam locomotive or a Brontosaurus. I still look forward to September every year, when Lake Atlantic wakes and shakes. I firmly believe that Tom Morey, inventor of the bodyboard, is one of the greatest benefactors to humanity in history; for like Gutenberg, the inventor of the printing press, he made available to the many a great pleasure that had once been the province of the few. For before Gutenberg, books were only for the rich; and before Morey, surfing was only for athletes.

Every kid looks forward to Christmas, but I looked forward even more to the two weeks each summer when we went to Ocean Grove, on the Jersey Shore. Like the Oak Bluffs "campground" in Martha's Vineyard (where we bought a tiny "gingerbread" cottage in 1999), it was founded in the nineteen century by Methodists as a religious retreat center and contained hundreds of colorful gingerbread houses and hotels.

In addition to the anonymously religious and almost mystical experience of riding powerful waves (for which surfers have their own distinctive term: "stoke"), my two other strongest childhood memories from Ocean Grove were also religious. One was hearing a sermon, at the age of about twelve, on Ecclesiastes, the most philosophical book in the Bible, and the question it raised about the "meaning of life", or what philosophers call the *summum bonum*, or greatest good. It was the first time I confronted a philosophical question, and I was hooked. For there is nothing more wasteful than an answer without a question, even a beautiful and elaborate answer, if the question is not asked and cared about. The whole of the Bible now appeared to me as an answer to Ecclesiastes, and my religion now appeared to me with a new luster and light. The preacher used the word "philosophy" to describe that issue, or that question, and I announced to my father that I wanted to be a philosopher. He replied something like, "You already are."

Another sermon I heard there was very powerful and passionate. (Protestants are definitely superior to Catholics in three things: sermons, hymns, and familiarity with the Bible.) It was by an old, retired preacher, and it was about his four most beloved chapters in the Bible. They were John 3, John 17, Romans 8, and 1 Corinthians 15. Not Matthew 5–7, the "Sermon on the Mount", or 1 Corinthians 13, on love, which are very beautiful and popular but which are about what we are supposed to do but don't do; these four, in contrast, were about what God gloriously did do. The preacher's heart and his honest and passionate love of those chapters did for my heart what the other preacher's philosophical take on Ecclesiastes did for my mind: it cast a new light on the whole of my religion. It turned these chapters into songs, to be endlessly sung and enjoyed; mysteries to be relished rather than problems to be solved. In fact it did that to life itself.

My father gave me a powerful and memorable lesson one pre-teen Christmas when I lusted mightily after a new bright orange Union Pacific diesel Lionel passenger train set. I kept dropping persistent hints about it to my parents. One day my father sat me down and explained that this was a very expensive present and that Santa Claus (which we all knew was him, but we still played the game) might not be able to afford it. I was crestfallen. Then he asked, "Do you know why we have Christmas?" "Sure, Dad. It's when Jesus was born." "Right. And why do we give each other gifts on Christmas?" "Because Jesus was the gift God gave us." "Right again. And why did God do that?" "Because he loves us." "Right again! So why do we give each other gifts?" "Because we love each other." The answers were easy and obvious to anyone except an academic theologian. "Very good, son. I'm very happy that you know that. Now if I can't afford to buy you that expensive train set, do you still know how much I love you?"

Ouch. I was afraid this would happen: a curveball after all those straight fastballs, and I couldn't hit curveballs. So I quickly tried to reason it out in my mind: Which answer would be more likely to get me the train set, a Yes or a No? Could I play the guilt game with him and hold him hostage to my love for that train? The answer wasn't clear to me, so I gave up, remembering the rule: When in doubt, tell the truth. So I answered, "Yeah, Dad, I know you love me." "Thanks, son; that means a lot to me. You've made me very happy." I thought: "Darn it, *he* didn't make *me* very happy. I gave the wrong answer. I let him off the hook. Now I won't get the train set." Well, I did get the train set, but I also got something much better. The train set is in my attic rusting away, but the memory of that lesson is still chugging down my tracks.

I have always loved the extraordinary, partly because I was easily bored by the ordinary. (I didn't know I had ADD then.) I read all the Superman and Batman comics I could, and, later, plenty of fantasy and science fiction. (Ray Bradbury was my favorite.) A book was to me another world, like Alice's rabbit hole. And words were not labels, but music. In high school I found poetry easy to remember, inspiring to recite (i.e., sing), and even fun to compose. My compositions were, of course, embarrassingly bad, but I was too young to be embarrassed. Poetry was much more like singing than like talking.

Later, when I discovered the poetry of Anglican, Orthodox, and Catholic liturgical languages, they tasted like fine wines, not only to my aesthetic taste but also to my deeper hunger for the joy and beauty that I unconsciously felt lacking in my Calvinist style of Christianity, even though I was convinced of its truth and goodness. The lyrics were profoundly true and good, but the melodies were not profoundly beautiful. And the architecture was frugal, utilitarian, and rational rather than expansive, Romantic, and mystical.

I don't believe that beauty is more important than truth and goodness, but I know it is more subjectively powerful; it is usually the first ambassador God sends us when He visits our souls, the point of the arrow that first pierces the target of the heart. Even truth and goodness attract our spirit because they are inspiringly true and good, when His Spirit, His breath, like wind, raises waves on the sea of our souls. We smell the beauty of His breath before we see the beauty of His truth or feel the beauty of His love. The words *ruah* in Hebrew and *pneuma* in Greek both have the triple meaning of breath, wind, and spirit.

෨ ෨ ෨

I got a D in "conduct" for pranks (most of which were so stupid that I can't remember what they were) and for "talking back" in third grade. I was so naïve that I found it hard to believe that not everyone felt grateful to be corrected when they were intellectually wrong. I got the lowest grade of anyone in my sixth grade class in "shop" (mainly woodworking and metalworking). All my blood seemed to go to my head instead of my hands. I nearly flunked both Advanced Algebra and Chemistry in high school (I remember my frustration when the teacher and the textbook didn't match.) I had to drop out of "French without Textbooks" in college (since I had both ADD and auditory processing problems but didn't know it), but I got straight A's in almost every other course I ever took without "sweating it". However, success through native intelligence instead of effort has its moral downside. I am lazy and lack courage and perseverance. I'm tough in thought and imagination but not in will, which is much more important. The simple key to the whole meaning of life, which is to become a saint, is not "Thy ideas be thought" or "Thy creativity be imagined" but "Thy will be done."

Computer language has always been adamantly incomprehensible and wildly frustrating to me. It finds no holding places in my mind. I am so bored with it that I cannot work up the will to master it. It has no color, it is all black and white, or gray, the dullest of all colors and the most popular of all colors today for cars. (I fear that eccentrics, curmudgeons, and nonconformists in every field are rapidly dying out.) Sometimes I dream of going on wild Luddite rages, smashing computers with axes and baseball bats. I cannot forgive Bill Gates for his invention of the torture chamber called Microsoft Word; and although my namesake Saint Peter was promised that the gates of Hell would not prevail, the Hell of Gates has prevailed against this Peter.

૨ ૨ ૨

The profoundest religious idea I ever had came to me one Sunday morning as we were riding home from church. I think I was about eight or nine years old. I remember exactly where we were: Haledon Avenue, corner of North Eighth Street. I said to my father, "Dad, I don't understand some of the stuff they teach us in Sunday school, and I don't understand some of the stuff in the pastor's sermons, but I think all that stuff, all those different things that we're supposed to learn in church—it's all just one thing, really, isn't it?" My father looked at me with a frown: "Just one thing? No, it's many things, many important things. Why do you think it's only one thing?" I replied, "Well, all we have to do is to ask God what he wants us to do and then do it, right?" I remember how my father's frown turned to a smile of approval and even pride. "You know, you're absolutely right, son. You're absolutely right." As a philosopher, I've had thousands of other ideas since then, and most of them were true and good, I hope, but as far as the primacy and profundity of an idea is concerned, it's all been downhill since that day.

I have never rejected any Christian dogma, whether as a Calvinist or as a Catholic, nor have I even had a serious crisis about its truth; but I have also never been secure and satisfied by my grasp of the dogmas I believed, whether as a Calvinist or as a Catholic. The very first original philosophical and theological conviction I remember having, very early—as soon as I went to Sunday school—was that there absolutely *had* to be much, much more to it—more to Christianity, more to life, more to the universe, more to objective reality—than I or my teachers or anyone else knew.

In college, when I discovered Plato with his doctrine of the transcendent Forms, Ideas, or archetypes, the "other world" outside the Cave, I recognized that world instantly. It was the world of what I most deeply sought, not just with my mind—not just "universals" or class concepts—but with my heart, which "has its reasons that the reason does not know" (Pascal). After all, "the big Idea" for Plato was not just "the True" but "the Good", which was also "the Beautiful".

I wondered whether the Platonic Forms were in fact angels, as in Charles Williams' mystical fantasy novel *The Place of the Lion*. Angels have always fascinated me: they are the true extraterrestrials, and they have never been successfully captured in even the greatest human art. The only even remotely satisfying verbal descriptions of them that I have ever discovered in print are in C. S. Lewis' chapter "The Descent of the Gods" in *That Hideous Strength*, the "Great Dance" at the end of his *Perelandra*, and "the Music of the Ainur" in Tolkien's creation myth in the first chapter of his *Silmarillion*.

My two primary teachers in religion at an early age were my father and Rev. Theodore Jansma, our well-read, wise, and patient pastor, who first introduced me to C. S. Lewis. As I have mentioned, my father was a very smart engineer who worked his way up from errand boy to the Chief Engineer of Morrison Machine Company. I was not interested in designing, making, or fixing complex industrial machines, but I respected his intelligence and expertise, which seemed to extend beyond machines to almost everything. He was also a good teacher, both by example and by words, and for a long time he seemed to me to have answers to all of my many questions, including questions about our Faith. But I remember three occasions as a pre-teen when my questions stumped him.

One was about the size of our denomination, the Reformed Church in America. I had learned in Sunday school about other Christian denominations, and I asked my father how large ours was, and the answer was "about a quarter of a million people in America". Then I asked how many other Christians there were in America and in the whole world, and the answer was many, many millions. Then I asked him why there were so many different Christian denominations, and why we disagreed with all the others. Instead of going into theological controversies, my father wisely answered that what all Christian denominations agreed on (basically, the Apostles' Creed) was much more important than what we disagreed about. But I persisted, "But we're right and they're wrong about those other things, right? Because if we're not, then we ought to change and join whatever denomination is right, right?" "Well, yes, and that's why we're in our denomination." "But how could God let all the others be wrong and only our one little denomination be all right?" He had no answer. He replied that "There are good Christians in every denomination", but that didn't answer my question.

I knew that the biggest "denomination" by far was Catholicism, and we thought that was the worst one of all, so I was a bit upset and confused about why the Holy Spirit had done His work so badly in taking care of His churches. But I didn't pursue the Catholic question. I thought their errors, as I understood them, were very obvious and stupid, like worshipping Mary and saints and statues and the pope and a little piece of bread, and Jesus being sacrificed over and over again in the Mass, and thinking you could buy your way into Heaven with a big enough merit pile of good works. It was unbelievable that they should believe what was so unbelievable. The fact that my father had no answer to my question about denominations opened my mind a bit to the other Protestant denominations, but not to Catholicism, which was "beyond the pale".

A second unanswered question concerned the theory of evolution. I wondered why it was said to be impious. I thought: God does most of the things He does in this universe gradually, and through natural laws, so why not the evolution of our bodies? I was surprised that my father had apparently never thought about that question, and he was shocked that I should be open to this "heresy". I still wonder why almost all who oppose that theory even when it is confined to a strictly biological level are Protestants and not Catholics.

The third question I asked my father, as a pre-teen, that he could not answer came up in Saint Patrick's Cathedral in New York City. As we lived just eighteen miles from the George Washington Bridge, we visited the city often in the forties and fifties. It was pretty clean and safe then, and full of just about everything interesting, and one of these was Saint Patrick's Cathedral. Calvinist churches, like Calvinists, are frugal, plain, humble, comfortable, unpretentious, and homey. I had never been in a cathedral before, and as soon as I stepped inside, I felt I had entered another universe. It was glorious, elaborate, mysterious, proud, pompous, pretentious, wonderful, and otherworldly. The German word *unheimlich* comes to mind, with connotations of "ghostly" as well as "not homely", "not familiar". It was extraordinarily extraordinary. I thought that this must be what Heaven looked like. It was literally miraculous, it was supernatural, it was not of this world.

I turned to my father and asked, "Dad, this is a *Catholic* church, isn't it?" "Yes." "And the Catholics are all wrong about their religion, right?" "Right. Very wrong." "Then why are their churches so beautiful?" Implicitly, I was asking about the unity of the transcendentals Truth, Goodness, and Beauty. How could they be opposed? How could Catholics' false and evil religion be so much more spectacularly beautiful than our true and good one?

The fact that my father had no answer was part of my answer. Of course I did not promptly convert then and there, or even dream of ever converting; it was just an unanswerable puzzle that God had led me to plant in the back of my mind where dark but fertile things grow. Why had God allowed the throne room of the Queen of Heaven to be owned by the Whore of Babylon? But the cathedral was a reality, it was data, it was unarguable. There are arguments against great truths and great goods but there are no arguments against great beauty. My heart was open to conversion long before my mind or my will. For the heart is more vulnerable than the head. It has no password or pin number. Its door cannot be locked. It is like water that seeps under the castle walls and past the guards even when the drawbridge is up, or like Bilbo the Hobbit, who creeps past Smaug the watchful dragon to steal his hoard of gold.

Later, the same thing was going to happen to me with Palestrina's music. It was not just more beautiful music than any I had ever heard, it was of a different order: transcendent, supernatural, in another dimension. It was an echo of Eden. It was angel music.

The religious music in which I had grown up and which had grown into my bones as a growing child had not been the present-day embarrassingly-*nice*, sweet, mindless, limp-wristed sexless schlock from the Saint Louis Jesuits. I call that sexless because it erases what the Bible called "the image of God" (Gen 2:15), viz. male and female, since it erases both Mars and Venus, both masculinity and femininity, both delicacy and strength. I think it is partly but significantly responsible for "the faithful departed" from the pews, since the psychological image of Jesus Christ suggested by those syrupy anti-hymns is as far from Christ Himself as a wet noodle is from a lion. And that is the aesthetic Purgatory that most Catholics every Sunday either endure or, worse, actually like, but do not sing. So my musical expectations were high, not low, when I heard Palestrina. I had never heard those embarrassingly shallow kindergarten yells called "praise choruses" that are so loved by megachurches and white Baptists (but not Black!). The lyrics are insultingly infantile even by the standards of a five year old, and whose "soft rock" score sounds like soft rocks scoring. As for "Christian rock", it is an embarrassing insult to rock as well as to Christianity. I miss the great old Protestant hymns, and I thank the Holy Spirit for sneaking many of them into many Catholic hymnbooks nowadays.

My point is that from the earliest age I had high standards for religious music. We Calvinists sang seventeenth- and eighteenth-century hymns whose strong melodies were fitting for their strong biblical lyrics that were turned into good poetry by the likes of Isaac Watts, John and Charles Wesley, and John Newton and set to music from Bach, Handel, and Haydn. But Palestrina and his ilk were to them as eagles were to robins, Gondor to the Shire, or venison to tacos.

Later, I also came to love Gregorian chant, the archetypical Catholic liturgical music, which is as simple and spare as Baroque music is rich and full. But both are "sexy", that is, both very feminine (subtle, humble, inward) and very masculine (strong, clear, confident) at the same time. This music could be sung by real angels; the new limp-wristed hymns could be sung only by limp-wristed Hallmark greeting card angels or by Ned Flanders on *The Simpsons*. Palestrina's music was harmonious but not *nice*; sweet but not sugary, strong but not screamy. It was *formidable*, like cathedrals. It obviously came from the same place as they did.

Palestrina gave me a foretaste of the rapture I would hear with the ears of my resurrected body in Heaven, as Saint Patrick's gave me a foresight of what I would see with Heavenly, resurrected eyes. It was almost a kind of out-of-body experience. I remember a similar out-of-body experience I had when listening to a Beethoven symphony for the first time: at one point I felt the fear that I could never get back into my body because I had become that music.

I have had only one other semi-mystical out-of-body experience, some years later, while bodysurfing at Wildwood Crest on the Jersey Shore in swells that had been raised by hurricane waves the day before. I let the inter-swirling swells carry me wherever they omnipotently willed—which, by God's mercy to a brain-damaged idiot drugged by sea water, was eventually up onto the beach. But while I was in the dangerous swells and swirls, a syllogism almost killed me: I reasoned that I could not drown because I had become the ocean, and the one thing that can never drown in the ocean is the ocean. I have been an avid surfer (bodyboarder) ever since, and even wrote a semi-serious missionary tract (*I Surf Therefore I Am*) to convert everyone, from grommets to fogies, to this secular religion. It is the cheapest and most joyful secular approximation (from afar, of course) to mystical experience that I know.

Every experience that takes us out of ourselves is potentially religious, or analogously religious. This is true of negative as well as positive experiences. My terrifying dreams of the Devil and my vivid memory of the burning cows running through our backyard had also taken me out of myself but in the other direction. The thing we deeply want (and also fear) is a thing we cannot control. And this is wonderful as well as terrifying. Our deepest will is to lose our will. I think it is not sacrilegious to call it spiritual orgasm. It is one of the dimensions of the mystery hinted at in all the great religions: that the highest life the human spirit is capable of is a kind of self-transcendence or self-death. "Blow, blow, blow till I be / But the breath of the Spirit blowing in me."

We Calvinists were far too rationalistic to countenance such mysticism. Calvin himself was so rationalistic that he saw his signature doctrine, the sovereignty of God, in the form of predestination, as logically opposed to free will, unlike Saint Augustine, who embraced both halves of that great and paradoxical mystery.

I think there was also a hidden racist element in our anti-Catholicism. Catholics were dark, dirty, poor, uneducated, lazy, crooked, lusty, emotional, unpredictable, materialistic, and not to be trusted—like Italians or Spaniards. That was seldom explicitly said but often assumed or implied. Our typical image of the Spaniard had shifty eyes, a pointed beard, and a concealed stiletto, and turned the thumbscrews of the Inquisition. Our typical image of the Italian was that of either a Mafia crook or a beggar.

I never encountered, in any Calvinist I knew, the idea, popularized by Max Weber, that Calvinism fostered the work ethic by assuming that if you worked hard you would get rich and if you were rich you knew that you were favored by God and probably predestined to be saved. All the Calvinists I knew did indeed have a very strong work ethic, but it had nothing to do with predestination, going to Heaven, or even with getting rich. In fact they treated money as Victorians treated sex: with embarrassment. The poor often try to pretend to be rich, but Dutch Calvinists, if they were rich, pretended to be poor. As with the Amish, "plain" was a compliment.

Their work ethic did have something to do with spiritual safety: idle hands were subject to the Devil's alluring temptations. Leisure and contemplation were not concepts of admiration but of suspicion. Thus Pieper's classic *Leisure: the Basis of Culture*, which I read before I read any explicitly Catholic books, was already a psychological "conversion" for me. I came to admire monks and monasteries, loved Thomas Merton's *Seven Storey Mountain*, and after my conversion seriously contemplated becoming a contemplative monk (but a Dominican, not a Trappist). My motives were not wholly pious. I find asceticism (e.g., fasting) rather onerous, and study and writing delightful and easy. I am not adept at or interested in most forms of physical work, and I am amazingly inept at every kind of technology. I think God gave everyone both an unusual talent, to discourage despair, and an unusual handicap, to discourage pride.

When I read Saint John of the Cross as a teenager, although I did not comprehend it, I "just knew" this mysticism was not "founded in mist, centered in 'I' and ending in schism" but was a great mountain of truth and goodness and beauty even though it was Catholic and therefore to be suspected. It was Saint Patrick's Cathedral in words. Among mountains it was Everest. I could not live on its heights, but I could be in awe of them.

4

High School Highs and Lows

We spend our four most difficult and crucial teenage years in what we call "high school". It is an ironic name, like "the Enlightenment".

"The Enlightenment" is an ironic name because its founders applied that "morning" name to what was in fact an "evening" thing, the dying of the greatest light, the Sonset of divinely revealed religion in the West, and the emergence, in its place, of the sad, shallow simplifications of, first, scientific reductionism and a rationalism that led to skepticism and, then, atheism, materialism, relativism, subjectivism, utilitarianism, deconstructionism, and nihilism. So naturally, the "Father of Lies" (Jn 8:44) inspired his dupes to call this endarkenment "the Enlightenment". As one of his high priests noted in *Mein Kampf*, people will believe "the Big Lie" more readily than little lies.

"High school" is similarly named ironically, for it was not a high point but a low point for me, as it was almost bound to be since its inhabitants are teenagers. Teenagers are borderline human beings with their brains not in their heads but in their hormones or their smartphones; confused know-it-alls, dogmatically skeptical; spoiled brats who see their free gift of education as an imposed prison sentence. That is an exaggeration and a joke, of course, but if it weren't at least 49 percent true, it wouldn't be funny at all.

When I graduated from Kossuth Street Elementary School in Haledon, my parents gave me the choice of going to the very large public Central High in downtown Paterson, where most of my friends from elementary school were going, or to the tiny, crowded Eastern Christian High School on the main street of Prospect Park, where all my new friends would be Christians, Calvinists, and Dutch. I was surprised that they gave me that momentous free choice at that early stage in my life. But I know now, as I did not then, that they gave me that choice only because they knew me well enough to be confident that even then my Christian identity was more important to me than my school friends, so that I would choose the Christian school, which I did.

I was a committed Christian, but I was not particularly pious. In fact, reflecting on all my teachers and courses at ECHS for four years, the courses of which I have no memories at all were the Bible courses, which we took every semester. I remember neither feelings of interest nor boredom, neither gratitude nor rebellion, neither skepticism nor edification. Yet I must have learned a lot. I suppose I remember nothing of it simply because I found it to be what I had expected, like the cycles of nature, rather than something remarkable and fascinating that upset the natural order, like a hurricane.

I won a prize in senior year for an anti-Catholic essay on Dostoevsky's "The Grand Inquisitor", which I misinterpreted as an attack on the Church and its "spiritual totalitarianism". It was rabble-rousing rhetoric, and it was wrong, but it was pretty potent propaganda. (A propa ganda is the propa mate for a propa goose.)

The single school building at ECHS was old, crowded, ramshackle, and even partially rotting, though clean. (The Dutch are probably the cleanest people in the world.) The lab, gym, auditorium, and playing field were all too small. In my senior year, the school moved to a much larger new campus in North Haledon, near the woods, and though I appreciated the improvements, I missed the closeness and comradery of the old place. The poor are always closer to each other than the rich are.

I remember my first day on the old campus. I knew absolutely no one and felt very anxious and uncomfortable, but I was surprised that no one laughed at me or bullied me, verbally or otherwise, and in fact one guy (Ted) deliberately reached out and befriended me. It felt more like an extended family than a prison or a workhouse.

I think my favorite class was music class. I had taken piano lessons for about eight years. I got up to grade 5 pieces (all classical; my favorite was Rimsky-Korsakov's *Scheherazade*), but I was too finger-clumsy and too soul-lazy to go any farther. My most vivid memory of my private piano lessons at home was being absolutely adamant about not turning off the radio during my lesson on the day in the fall of 1951 when my beloved New York Giants and their archenemies, the Brooklyn Dodgers, were in a one-game playoff. When

Bobby Thomson hit the walk-off home run that has ever since been known as "the shot heard 'round the world", I banged on the keyboard with unrestricted glee, jumped up, and refused to take the rest of the lesson. Great joy as well as great misery makes ordinary work not only trivial but impossible. The Giants then felt more gigantic than God to my imagination.

They were "our" Giants. The pronoun was to come back to haunt me with a laugh many years later when I became a Red Sox fan, had children, and habitually came back from Fenway Park happy when "we" won and unhappy when "we" lost. My three daughters all told me that when they were very young, they thought I actually played for the Red Sox. They also thought, when I told them that I was going to Boston College, where I've taught for over sixty years, that I was still a college student, now in my thirties, probably a very slow one.

My best teacher in high school was Mr. Van Til, who taught English, under whose wise guidance I fell in love with Shakespeare, the Romantic poets, and T.S. Eliot ("The Hollow Men" and "Prufrock"), but not with Milton, who sounded too pompous. Mr. Van Til encouraged my poetry writing habits and even my science fiction reading habits. Reading junky stories and junky newspapers (the *New York Daily News*) at least developed the habit of reading and expanded my consciousness. And reading fiction is travel: time travel, to past (historical novels) or future (science fiction), and travel in space, into the minds of other cultures and personalities. Some of my best friends are imaginary.

I loved my Latin teacher, whose face and voice were as clear and beautiful as the music of the Latin language itself. So even though I was lazy and did *not* love the vast amounts of memorizing, I did love how the results sounded on my lips. Surely no language is more like music than Latin.

Our gym teacher, Barney Steen, was both tough and tender, demanding and understanding. He later moved to Calvin College and won a couple of basketball championships there. Our playing field at the old ECHS was too small for baseball or softball, but we did play "tag" or "tail" football, for which I designed some plays but successfully executed none. We played intramural basketball in the three-quarter-size gym, and I was tall enough to score some points in the paint and fast enough to do some runaway fast breaks, but so hopelessly clumsy that I kept dribbling off my shoes. But we were taught strategy and sportsmanship, so it was intellectual and moral as well as physical education.

My math teacher showed me great patience and attention when I demonstrated that the structures of my mind did not match the structures of mathematical realities. I habitually got the right answers by the wrong methods (not cheating) and the wrong answers by the right methods. (I do the same now with computers.) My chemistry teacher did not have such patience, and I emerged with a barely passing D in that course. Nor did my no-nonsense, no-patience geometry teacher, who was an ex-marine. I remember such great frustration in that course that I tore my geometry textbook in half and threw it at the wall. But in college, in Greek philosophy I read Euclid on my own with delight rather than frustration. It was logic, after all, and that is the structure and strategy of philosophy.

I was given the choice to take either typing or World Literature, and my parents and teachers persuaded me to choose typing (even though I wanted the other course), either because they saw in me a future writer or, more likely, simply because it was more practical. My typing teacher was a fat, genial man who in his day had played professional baseball (he was the second-string catcher for the Detroit Tigers). He was not very smart, but he was our hero for his stories and jokes.

I played Board 1 (top player) on our Chess Club, and we competed against other, larger schools, winning about half the time—which was gratifying because we were always the underdogs. When I began teaching at Boston College, I played competitive chess there the first year, and we won a championship in a league that included Harvard and MIT. But the pressure and anxiety were so agonizing and debilitating to me that I was no longer having fun and was losing sleep after losses, so I gave it up.

I was also part of an a capella quartet in high school. All four of us played different instruments and loved music, including country-western, folk songs, and Black spirituals. We became close friends and often double, triple, or quadruple dated. Henry, who was a year older, was the only one with a car: a big, black, long, six-passenger '32 Chevy, with a very large dent in the front fender, into which he put flowers to impress the girls.

My first car was a 1940 Ford with a stick shift. As a freshman, I was driven to school by an older kid, a neighbor, who hit 95 mph on narrow country roads. I didn't want to get him in trouble, but I told my parents I couldn't risk my life by getting into his car again. Another friend, another speeder, cracked up his brand new bright red convertible, barely survived, and had to take a year off from school to heal all the many broken bones. Much later in life, after I had four kids and bought a maroon Buick Roadmaster to hold them all, another philosopher won an argument with me about free will versus determinism by asking me what color my car was and claiming that he could explain that choice deterministically. He asked me what past cars I remembered best, and I answered, "The one my friend the speedster had for the shortest time and the one my father had the longest time." "And what colors were they?" "My friend's was bright red and my father's was tan." "And what did you think of your friend?" "I liked him but he was a risk-taker." "And what did you think of your father?" "A very good man but a little too conservative." "See? Maroon is the perfect blend of bright red and dull tan. That wasn't as free a choice as you thought." That conversation taught me something: not that our choices are *determined* rather than free, but that they are *conditioned* more than we suspect by forces we do not recognize.

Although I never had a crisis of faith or a desire to rebel against Christianity's creeds (as distinct from its commandments), I was more "into" pranks than into prayer and felt more joy in jokes than in Jesus. "Pranks" was the nickname my friends called me (later turned into "Pratz" by a kid with auditory processing problems).

I was a prankster from childhood. At the age of about six, I tried to put a small bucket of water on top of my bedroom door to fall on my mother when she opened the door; it did not work except to merit me The Paddle. In elementary school I always got A's and B's on my report card in every other subject except "shop", but C's and D's in "conduct" or "deportment". In high school chemistry lab after class I experimented with some foaming, evil-looking purple mixture containing potassium chromate, which, when ignited, burned through the stainless steel top of the new lab table. I was never caught, was never asked about it (I would have confessed), and never paid for the damage. We also pranked the kid who was the easiest to scare by slipping a non-toxic chemical into his soda that turned his pee blue, which we had researched as being a possible symptom of a fatal condition; then, seeing him pee blue in the boys' bathroom and pretending concern, we looked it up with him in the medical encyclopedia. The result was terror and more blue pee, in his pants. Our laughter probably saved his sanity.

I was actually expelled from (high) school for a day because of a prank. After classes, I had scrawled on the blackboard some cartoon figures of some of our teachers, with silly captions (some rhyming). I thought it was all in good fun, but Mr. Beversluis, the principal, expelled me from school the next day and demanded to speak to my mother (in our home!). At the interview, I said I was sorry and would not do it again. But his large private wink to me on his way out told me that he had only been doing his duty and had actually found my cartoons quite funny, including the one with him as the Mad Hatter from *Alice in Wonderland* (he had a long, craggy face, a pointed nose, and very large ears).

To prepare for my role as Hamlet in our senior play, I had to take fencing lessons for the last scene, where Hamlet and Laertes kill each other in a duel with a poisoned rapier. To elicit the blood, I was directed to put catsup in a plastic bag under my armpit, tear a small hole in the costume there and in the bag, and squeeze the fake blood out while fencing. During dress rehearsal the fake worked very well, but during the performance there was so much "blood" on the floor that in the subsequent fighting I tripped on it and slid (like Jackie Robinson stealing second base) into the cardboard castle walls that were our set, literally bringing down the house. I had invented a new ending for the play!

5

Calvin College: Campus Life

Calvin College in 1955 was a small liberal arts college of fifteen hundred students in Grand Rapids, Michigan. Tuition was $250 per semester. The campus consisted of five classical colonial brick buildings sitting on a suburban city block within walking distance of downtown. There was only one dormitory building, for freshmen boys only, with spartan, monastic rooms (two to a room, with bunk beds and cork floors). Girls rented rooms in private houses near campus for all four years, boys for three. The only two large buildings were (1) the administration building, whose basement contained the offices of the student newspaper, the *Chimes*, on which I worked as an editor and writer, and (2) the auditorium and chapel, which required thrice-weekly attendance for all students. I remember many laughs chiming from the *Chimes* office but none from the chapel, which ought to have had more chimes of joy, not fewer. Selected students were occasionally invited to give short speeches in chapel, and my turn became notorious, as I found out years later. I argued that Socrates was not only the greatest philosopher (as Saint Thomas Aquinas said) but also an anonymous Christian (as Saint Justin Martyr said), and almost certainly a saint in Heaven, as Erasmus implied when he famously wrote, "Saint Socrates, pray for us." (Later, some of my friends and colleagues at Boston College and Gordon College formed the "Saint Socrates Society".)

Formal and disciplined schools usually attract pranks and pranksters; "progressive" and permissive schools usually do not. A few days into my first semester, my roommate read that if a sleeper's hand is immersed in warm water, he will pee in bed. He waited until I was asleep, performed the prank, and got no result at all. So he simply doused me with the bucket of water. (Why waste water?) I was not angry at the bath, but at the lack of cleverness of this "prank", so I

48

found a lizard and put it in his bed under the covers the next evening. His reaction on going to bed was a gratifying terror. Every night after that, he made "lizard check" before going to bed.

I was the campaign manager for our candidate for class president the first year. He lost the election by a large margin, despite (or, more probably, because of) his cleverness. He opened his campaign speech with: "They say a good speech should begin with a bang, so ..." and then took out a realistic looking plastic gun and shot it. What was inside was not a bullet but a red flag that came out and read "Bang!" The students were, somehow, not impressed by this piece of advanced intelligence. Nor by the wonderful sound of our large pumpkins smashing on the sidewalk when dropped from our dorm's second-story windows to interrupt the opposing candidate's outdoor campaign speech.

I am not good at organizing real things and people, only ideas. In eighth grade, the class had voted for me for class president, and I declined because I feared business, responsibility, and publicity. So I was made class treasurer, in charge of fundraising events. At the end of the year, my teacher told me, "I've been teaching here for almost fifty years, and you are the only class treasurer who not only made no money for the class but actually lost some." When I tried selling cosmetics door to door during the summer to help with my college tuition, the only people who ever bought any were my relatives.

My best prank was not the cat food my roommate and I served on crackers as hors d'ouvres at a party (which was actually praised by one victim) but probably the two-minute long pee in a bathroom that was separated from the living room only by a decorative hanging, so that everything in the bathroom could be heard, including peeing. I overheard that the guests were betting money on who peed the longest, as timed by a timer outside the bathroom; so I found a very large balloon (a small weather balloon, I think), sneaked it into the bathroom deflated, filled it with water, and when I went to pee kept dripping it into the toilet for two whole minutes. Looks of wonder and worship appeared on faces when I emerged.

Our best collective prank was the whole dormitory's prank on the most naïve student among us, who was seriously obsessed with his idea that the world was coming to an end soon. His theory was that one morning the sun simply would not come up. So we all agreed to secretly set all the clocks in the dorm, including his alarm, forward three hours. We all got up at 4 A.M., when the clocks said it was 7, dressed, washed, and walked with him across campus toward the dining hall. It was 7:30, and there was no sunlight. He was terrified, totally convinced that this was the Last Day, and even more so when we all pooh-poohed the idea. The best pranks always cost something, in this case three hours' of our sleep.

A real terror for all of us came on another day when a large tornado clearly appeared on the horizon. It touched down only about ten miles away. Next to the hurricane (Carol, 1954), it was the most delightfully scary thing I had ever seen.

Also scary were the stories two serious students from Sri Lanka (then Ceylon) told of seeing evil spirits materializing and manifesting. They had seen pagan priests somehow, with the aid of "the spirits", producing the vision of body parts flying through the air at people, bodies without heads walking, and heads without bodies flying. These two students were both pre-seminary students who were training to be missionaries to their homeland. To get credibility there, they knew they also had to be exorcists. I had thought that only Catholics did that.

One student, whose father was a professional stage magician, had a gift of ESP that I tested by making the five cards Dr. Rhine used for his experiments at Duke (dot, circle, square, triangle, cross), putting myself at the near corner of a large, darkened room and him at the far corner, and having him "guess" which card I was looking at. He got twenty-one out of twenty-one. When I reversed it by mentally "receiving" the images of the five cards from him, I got ten out of twenty-one. I'm convinced it was not just stage magic and trickery. We all have a little bit of mental telepathy, I think; that's why, when we stare at someone ahead of us in line or on a bus, that person nearly always feels it and looks back at us. But some people have more than others of that gift, as of other gifts. And of course there are also both fakes and dangers there, as everywhere.

The fifties were far from perfect, but they were Eden compared to the about-to-come Sexual Revolution. The guys at Calvin, as everywhere else, were often crude braggarts and chauvinists in speech but not usually in action. But like all guys, we were shallow. John Donne wrote, "Look not for mind in women." He was wrong, of course, but if he had added "pretty" before "women", he would have been almost right. One seldom-confessed secret is that almost all men are suckers for a pretty face. Until they get older, they cannot seriously fall in love with ugly or even ordinary-looking women. I dated very rarely because I found the girls at Calvin boring either in mind or body. God apportions His gifts very parsimoniously; perhaps He is a Dutch Calvinist.

Evidence for that theological opinion at Calvin included the fact that breakfast in the student dining hall offered us the choice between bacon *or* eggs. The food in the dining hall reflected the architecture: it was Spartan and spare, not Athenian and abundant. Dutch Calvinists make Scotchmen look like wasteful profligates. But they know it and joke about it. E.g., How can you tell a Dutch house? By the paper plates on the clothesline.

Not until senior year were we allowed to have cars. Once, after a disappointing date, I drove out into the country to one of my favorite contemplative spots, next to a wooded lake about five miles from campus. It had rained a lot, and the car got stuck in the lakeside mud. The more I tried to exit the mud, the more I entered it. Eventually the car was in muddy water over a foot deep. It was after midnight, and no tow service was available, so I left the car there and walked back to campus in the rain. Shortly after I had gone to bed and fallen asleep, at about 3 A.M., I was awakened by a phone call from my mother, in New Jersey. She said, "Peter, I'm sorry to call you at this hour, but somehow I think you're in some kind of trouble. What happened?" Mothers by nature have preternatural gifts.

One Thanksgiving, three of us were driving home from Grand Rapids to New Jersey, and there was black ice on the Pennsylvania Turnpike. Our driver hit a patch of the ice, and the car spun around like a breakdancer and came to rest right in the middle of the highway, across the two lanes, stalled. The driver could not get the car started. Another car approached, hit the same patch of ice, and slid toward us, sideways. There seemed to be no room for him to pass us on either side, and he could not stop. The other passenger and I ran out of the car and jumped over the guardrail, but the driver heroically (or stupidly) stayed inside the car trying to start it. The approaching car, totally out of control, miraculously (?) straightened out and slid through the tiny space between our car and the guardrail that we had jumped over. Another, invisible Driver had apparently taken the wheel.

My roommate, Bill Brown, who was the most terrible driver I ever had the misfortune to drive with, was also one of the best punsters I· ever met. He had all his stuff from his bedroom at home in California shipped to his apartment at Calvin *except* his collection of art prints, just so that each day he could say "Some day my prints will come." Bill was large, ursine, eccentric, smart, and messy. He never cleaned his room or even put his things away because, he claimed, no one had ever given him a logically valid proof that he had to do it. (In fact, no one ever tried to!) As we shall see later, the theological question that he posed to me merely as a thought experiment on the first day I met him was what inadvertently started me on my road to investigating Catholicism. (It was "Why don't we pray to saints like Catholics do?" My answer, "Because we're not Catholics", was deservedly shredded by his logic: "We don't do that because we're not Catholics, and we're not Catholics because we don't do that" is, of course, arguing in a circle.)

Unlike many other philosophers and philosophy students, I had the usual male interest in sports, attending nearly every basketball game of the season when Calvin won the state championship. I still remember the names of the starting five: Newsome, Kok, Diekema, Vroon, Steen. Vroon shot both his free throws and what would today be his three-pointers with both hands and over his head. There was no shot clock then, and the worst team in the league, Olivet, almost beat us simply by keeping the ball interminably. They were good ball handlers and defenders but terrible shooters. The final score was something like 14–13, all their points coming on fouls.

I joined an intervarsity bowling league, and even though I was only an average bowler, I helped my team win first place because, in the final game, I asked the captain of the opposing team, who had the best average in the league, a simple question: "I've read a lot of books on bowling, and you do absolutely everything right. You have the best body language I've ever seen. But the one and only thing none of the books tell us is what to do with your left arm when you release the ball with your right. I'm looking forward to learning that from you and your perfect form tonight." Predictably, his attention was so diverted that we beat him. Getting in your own way mentally is as self-destructive as doing it physically—or morally. (Think about that for a minute!)

One of my best friends, Roger Verhulst, was so good at Monopoly that he competed in the finals of a national championship. He also taught me to play poker, and I won the very first time, against about half a dozen longtime players. It was the only time I ever won at poker.

The *Chimes* newspaper staff also invented a new game that we called "slunch". It stood for "Sam's lunch". Sam was a good-natured, clumsy newbie on our staff, and he took his lunch in a brown paper bag to school each day to eat during lunch break in the *Chimes* office. We would steal it, surround it with dozens of large rubber bands, and play keep-away with it throughout lunch hour, bouncing it off the wall to each other. Yes, it was silly, shallow, and selfish, but it was the only game we always won, and Sam the wannabe was grateful for the attention.

In addition to the *Chimes* newspaper, we once a year produced a satire of the local newspaper of our denomination, which was called *The Banner*. Ours was called *The Bananer*. Its slogan was: "Often in error, never in doubt." Like most kids, we loved comedy and satire, but it was all in fun, not hard, nasty, and angry like so many stand-up "comedians" today.

A patriarch of our denomination a generation ago in Holland had famously called dancing, moviegoing, and card playing "the Rubicon that no real Calvinist can cross." We did two of those three, but we never danced, not because we thought it was wicked, but because we were too clumsy.

Dutch Calvinists usually were teetotalers, but they smoked a lot. They were careful about their brain cells, but not about their lungs. I suspect we all have a double standard somewhere; we want to feel like moral heroes, but we also want to take moral vacations. To some people, human life is sacred in the womb and the gerontology ward but not so much in between. To other people, it's not OK to kill killers (they're against capital punishment), but it's OK to kill innocent human beings in the womb.

Contrary to official Calvin College policy, most of the students I knew drank beer, wine, and liquor. My favorite was single malt scotch, which was a fairly safe drink because you have to drink very slowly and delicately to savor it. But students never drank on campus,

and our off-campus parties were never "busted". We never saw drugs
or even heard of any students using them, and we seldom got really
drunk. One bad hangover was enough to deter me forever from the
misuse of that good thing which God invented "to gladden the heart
of man", according to the verse that Calvinists pretended was not in
the Bible.

6

Teachers

My teachers at Calvin (all of whom were members of the Christian Reformed Church and nearly all of whom were Dutch) included George Harper, who had been one of J.R.R. Tolkien's students at Oxford and who regaled us with tales about Tolkien's multiple eccentricities; Dr. Miller, a contrarian history professor who labeled himself "pro-Palestinian, anti-antiSemitic, and anti-Zionist"; Rev. Weidenaar, a wise and simple old Calvinist preacher who looked almost exactly like Gandalf; Dr. Timmerman, a charming, slow-speaking English professor who patiently outlined everything on the blackboard as he was simultaneously telling us gentle jokes; Dr. Van Til, a physics professor who made the history of science and the logical use of the scientific method a riveting drama; and Dr. Rienstra, a history professor who made the Catholic Middle Ages fascinating and attractive. Drs. Boersma and Fridsma made the German language almost fun.

For first-year Greek, we had a very large man whose name I have forgotten. He was tough and demanding but clear and understanding. He taught Greek as a drill sergeant teaches obedience, and he successfully forced us to master one of the world's most difficult languages but the incomparably best one for philosophy. It was sweat but sweet, hell but holy. It made the much easier "koine" (common) Greek of Mark's Gospel, which we went through word for word in second-year Greek, a cinch and a delight. Third year was Plato's "Apology", which unfolded like an orchid. I learned that philosophy and religion are both like poetry in that there is no way to translate their great texts into another language without losing many subtleties, distinctions, beauties, and implications.

I had a charming French teacher (Mr. Otten) whose total-immersion, no-textbook course was so frustrating that I had to drop

it or flunk it, even though I got straight A's in every other language
(Latin, German, Greek, and English, which is increasingly becoming
a foreign language today). His French course gave me the same kind
of frustration then that everything digital gives me today.

My first philosophy course was from Dr. Runner, a disciple of Her-
mann Dooyeweerd, a hyper-Calvinist in Holland who fit everything
in human existence into fourteen "anticipations and retrocipations",
and his colleague D.H.Th. Vollenhoven, who fit all philosophers in
history into categories even more all-encompassing and rationalistic
than Hegel. Yet both inveighed heartily against reason itself as fallen,
untrustworthy, and pagan. In Runner's course in Greek philosophy,
we didn't get to Socrates, Plato, and Aristotle until the last week. It
was all Dooyeweerd and Vollenhoven.

Runner was a true eccentric. He was too absentminded to drive
a car, jumped with shell shock whenever we dropped a textbook
on the floor, and sometimes lectured from a chair atop his desk
that he called his "throne". His greatest achievement, we thought,
was a prank: college rules said students had to wait ten minutes for
teachers when they were late, then they were free to leave; and
Runner once hid on a ledge outside our large classroom window
so that he could catch his class leaving the classroom before the ten
minutes had expired. He jumped into the room shouting "Geron-
imo! Gotcha!"

When I registered for sophomore courses, the professor asked me
what I thought about Dr. Runner's course that I had taken, and I
said, "I thought I'd like philosophy, but if that's philosophy, it's not
for me." He advised me not to give up on philosophy but to try Dr.
Jellema's course instead. I did, and when I went to Jellema's class, I
found that he was the professor who had registered me.

I loved Jellema's courses because he loved the philosophers, especially the classics. I took one course from him every semester from
then on. He is the primary reason I am a philosopher. Alvin Plant-
inga and Nick Wolterstorff, two of the best Christian philosophers of
our era, were also his students at Calvin. Like Socrates, Jellema never
wrote a book, but he asked the most searching Socratic questions
of us in class. In many ways, he contrasted our "typically modern"
beliefs with those of classical philosophers, and it was usually a contrast
between the shallow, narrow, and reductionistic versus the profound,

broad, and full. His course in medieval philosophy made me a Thomist before I had any serious thought of becoming a Catholic.

I also took a disappointingly formulaic course on Thomistic metaphysics at the local Catholic college, Aquinas College, which taught me why so many Catholic schools were abandoning textbook Thomism. It was full of formulas that we had to memorize even if we did not comprehend them, and the exam did not test understanding so much as Thomistic orthodoxy. I came to learn that Thomas was much more exciting than Thomists and much clearer than the Thomists who tried to clarify him. (I found Gilson and Maritain the two exceptions.)

Jellema's exam for his course on Augustine's *The City of God* (*De Civitate Dei*) was to come into the classroom, write on the board the single word *civitas* ("community" or "city") and say: "Write about that." (Exams were written on blackboards then, or duplicated with carbon paper or purple mimeograph paper. There were no photocopiers.) For his course in metaphysics, in which we had gone very deeply into Plato, Aristotle, Plotinus, Augustine, Aquinas, Descartes, Kant, and Hegel, he said simply: "You have three hours. Summarize the course." In his course in modern philosophy, he assigned Hume's *Enquiry Concerning Human Understanding* over a long holiday weekend (Thanksgiving or Easter). We were twelve philosophy majors, and we all remained on campus over the holiday and studied together. We simply could not refute Hume, even though we desperately wanted to, because his conclusion was a radical skepticism. But his premises seemed obvious and innocuous. When class met again, we confessed to Dr. Jellema that we had failed to find Hume's mistake and asked him to show us what it was. He refused, and explained, "I'm not a thief. I won't rob you of your work. Go back and find it yourself. You've taken logic; find the ambiguity, the false premise, or the logical fallacy." We did.

Jellema was very unlike Runner, but he was also the classic "absentminded professor". Once, when our teacher was late, Jellema entered our classroom instead of his by mistake, didn't recognize his error because he recognized some faces that were in his class, too, and began to lecture us. Our real teacher came in late and simply sat down in the back row. Jellema said, "Welcome" and went on with his lecture. It was so good that we did not interrupt, enlighten him, and embarrass him until the end of the class.

One of the best decisions in my life was not to take any courses in sociology or psychology. I loved all the humanities (philosophy, literature, theology, history), all the arts, and all the natural sciences (physics, astronomy, biology, and even chemistry, though I barely passed it), and admired math, though I was not good at it. But I was suspicious of what I thought were these two pseudosciences that claim to use the scientific method. That method works well to understand all the objects of human understanding but not Man, the subject. As Hingest, the tough-minded, skeptical chemist in C.S. Lewis' prophetic dystopian novel *That Hideous Strength*, put it, "You can't know people; you can only get to know them." It's the distinction other languages make, between "savoir" and "connaître" or between "wissen" and "kennen". I found numerous philosophical thinkers, all on the fringe of the philosophical establishment, who believed the same thing: Josiah Royce (*The Religious Aspect of Philosophy*), Joseph Wood Krutch (*The Measure of Man*), Neil Postman (*Technopoly*), Michael Polanyi (*Personal Knowledge, The Tacit Dimension*), William James (whose "pragmatism" seemed to me as different from John Dewey's as Saint Jude was from Judas) and all the Existentialists, both atheistic and theistic, especially Kierkegaard.

≥❧ ≥❧ ≥❧

I think I should tell you something about my failures and frustrations because it reveals something about my mind and my philosophy. I am the most astonishingly incompetent computer user in the world and am almost proud of it. There are simply no holding places in my mind for concepts in the digital universe. My computers trick me in astonishingly diverse and unpredictable ways. These so-called mere machines seem to be more cleverly creative and original than my students. They are not machines: machines are predictable. Push a button twice and you get the same reaction twice. Whatever computers I use seem to develop free will at my touch, for they have invented so many new and never-seen-before ways to drive me insane that I almost believe they are supernaturally inspired by the Unholy Spirit. What is far more predictable than my computers is the three formulas repeated by all the many techsperts (tech experts) to whom I come with my troubles: "I've never seen that before", 'I have no idea what is happening", and "It shouldn't be doing that."

I have an unbalanced brain. The intuitive half seems to block the calculating half. When I took the SAT and GRE exams, I got 100% on all the English and philosophy parts and nearly flunked the math parts. I remember nearly every poem and song I hear and love, but not numbers, which seem to me totally boring and empty of meaning. I remember telephone numbers either by translating them into letters or by remembering the *sounds* the numbers make when spoken. "Spoken" is for me close to "sung". Computers don't sing.

I was tempted by but did not succumb to both medieval (Scholastic) and modern (Hegelian) rationalism, and, probably in subconscious reaction, by the anti-rationalism of Kierkegaard, whom I regard as the greatest Protestant philosopher of all time. Our Kierkegaard teacher (Dr. Prins) had just discovered him, and his love and enthusiasm were contagious. Later, I took graduate courses on Kierkegaard both at Yale and at Fordham from world-renowned Kierkegaard experts, and they were both deeply disappointing compared to my undergraduate Calvin course from this unknown newbie. Philosophy is supposed to be "the love of wisdom", but many prestigious philosophers have lost both the wisdom and the love.

Though I love Socratic logic (and even wrote a book on it: the only full-length philosophical treatment of classical "Aristotelian" logic in print), my instinctive sympathies were always on the side of the more humane opponents of rationalism: Kierkegaard versus Hegel, Pascal versus Descartes, James versus Dewey, Marcel versus Sartre. I love Augustine's love of paradox. Nearly all Christian doctrines are paradoxes, e.g., our wills are really free *and* really destined (though not "pre") by God. Augustine is full of paradoxes because Christianity is full of paradoxes, and Christianity is full of paradoxes because life itself is, both at its beginning and at the end: we live in the world only by dying to the womb, and we live in Heaven only by dying to the world.

Another philosophy professor at Calvin, Dr. Orlebeke, gave me the hardest assignment I had ever had as my final paper: to outline logically C. S. Lewis' *The Abolition of Man* in detail. It is short, but it is probably Lewis' most difficult as well as his most important book. My outline took far more time, more re-reading, and more re-thinking than I had ever been required to do before. But it taught me how to really, really read a book. (I highly recommend Mortimer Adler's *How to Read a Book*, which sounds like a self-contradictory title because

it assumes that we can already read a book, since it is a book, but it
also assumes that we can't yet "really, really read" a book.)

C. S. Lewis' *The Problem of Pain* was the first book I read that I
did not fully understand at first reading but knew very clearly that
the fault was not in the author's wonderfully clear mind but in my
own. His *Mere Christianity* is incredibly clear and simple and at the
same time profound. It is one of the two books I always recommend
to anyone who wants to know what Christianity is. (The other one
is of course the New Testament.) *Mere Christianity* also saved the
dying faith of another roommate of mine, especially when he paired
it with Bertrand Russell's "Why I Am Not a Christian". His verdict
on Russell was: "Well, if that's the world's most brilliant atheist's
argument against being a Christian, I guess it's pretty clear that I have
got to be one."

Lewis became my very best teacher by a quirk of Divine Providence. After graduating from Calvin, my friend Roger Verhulst went
to work for William B. Eerdmans publishing company, which put out
a series of small books on "contemporary writers in Christian perspec-
tive". A few years after we both graduated, before I had published anything, Roger called me with an offer to write one of these books and to
pick my author. I picked Tolkien, and Roger said OK. But before the
contract came, another call from Roger came. "Peter, could you pick
another author? We just got a call from W. H. Auden, who is probably
the second greatest poet in the world, next to T. S. Eliot, and he wants
to write a book for us on Tolkien, whom he admires enormously. In
fact he said that if any critic does not love Tolkien, he cannot ever
again take him seriously. Now I know that you may become a more
famous poet than Auden some day, but you're not there yet, and we
very much want to sign Auden up for that book, so we don't want to
pass up that opportunity by giving you that contract I promised. But
we do want you to write one for us. So could you choose another
author? Any one."

I replied, "The only other author I admire as much as Tolkien is
C. S. Lewis. But I know he's written about thirty books, and I've
read only a few of them, so I need at least a year to read all the rest.
Can I have a contract for a book on Lewis with a two-year-long
deadline?" Eerdmans wanted one year, so we compromised on eighteen months, during which I read everything Lewis had published

and got to know him better than any other writer. And he's been in my head ever since.

Meanwhile, Tolkien, who was still living, got wind of the fact that Auden was writing a book on him and wrote a curmudgeonly letter to Eerdmans and another one to Auden complaining: "Can you not at least wait until my bones are in my grave before you disturb them?" Tolkien had not hesitated to insult a great poet; what would he have said about this brash American newbie daring to dissect his bones? God not only delivered me from that but also delivered me into Lewis and his mind with perfect providential timing.

As a matter of fact, *everything* is providential or else nothing is. God is not an interfering Zeus, a character in our drama, but the Author of it all. He is my real biographer, and everyone else's, too, but you can't read His corrections of my feeble attempts here until you get to Heaven and into His head.

7

Music and Liturgy

Music has always struck me as the most profound of all languages. I think it is likely that music is also first historically, first in time as well as rank. First came music; then came song, when words were added; then came poetry, when the words were separated from the music; then came prose, first eloquent, poetic prose, then prosaic prose; then came numbers; and then finally base-two, digital, computer language. That progression has always appeared to me rightly ordered, in a seven-step hierarchy. I was surprised and dismayed to discover that the accepted, standard theory among anthropologists is that the first language was numbers, used for purely practical reasons, for calculating the worth of goods to buy or sell; and that the more interesting and beautiful and mysterious the level of language was, the less primordial. Poetry was fancified prose, like icing on a cake; and music was poetry minus the words, like the icing without the cake.

No. In fact I believe there is available empirical evidence to suggest the opposite. Everywhere on earth, the language of "primitive" people and country people, not "advanced" city dwellers, is the most eloquent, poetic, musical, and beautiful. When my Boston neighbor came back from his first trip to his relatives in rural Tuscany and I asked him what impressed him most about Italy, he said, "They all talk like poets. They sing when they talk. But not so much in the city."

I believe that poetry is not ornamented prose; prose is fallen poetry. The most recent language, computer language, is of all languages the most "fallen", empty, meaningless, and boring. It is a language without any intelligence at all. In fact "artificial intelligence" is an oxymoron. It does not exist.

I was thrilled and instantly said "Amen" when I discovered my "reversed hierarchy", with music at the top, in Lewis' *The Magician's*

Nephew, in *The Chronicles of Narnia*, and in the "Ainulindalë" in Tolkien's *The Silmarillion*. Both authors see the world itself being created *in* music, *sung* into existence. Perhaps music was the universal language spoken in Eden and broken in pieces at Babel (Gen 11:1–9).

We might even extend the hierarchy one more level and say that language (language as such, and therefore all language, beginning with music) is not subordinate to things, but that things are subordinate to language: the language of the Mind of God (which Christian philosophers of the Middle Ages identified as the proper home of Plato's eternal "Ideas"). I found this view implied in Heidegger's description of language as "the House of Being" and in his oracular assurance in his *Introduction to Metaphysics* that "words and language are not wrappings in which things are packed for the commerce of those who write and speak. It is in words and language that things first come into being and are. For this reason the misuse of language in idle talk, in slogans and phrases, destroys our authentic relation to things." Though he was definitely not a Christian or even a theist, Heidegger knew that "in the beginning was the Word." In the Memphite Drama, the ancient Egyptian sacred story that is more than four thousand years old, the creator-god *speaks* the world into existence. He says "seas" and there are seas. He says "whales" and there are whales.

Although I loved music, I did not love discipline, but I agreed to take piano lessons in elementary school. I did not play well, but I loved the music. I was capable but lazy, and not interested in "practice makes perfect." I didn't know then, but discovered decades later, that I had ADD, which made me easily bored, which in turn made concentration difficult. But music itself never bored me.

Nor did voice practice, as distinct from piano practice. I was in an a capella quartet in high school (we were pretty good, if I do say so myself), and I joined the Oratorio Society at Calvin. I found that being *inside* Handel's "Messiah" and Haydn's "Creation" while singing these masterpieces with a large group in an acoustic auditorium is strikingly different from simply hearing others sing it, on recordings or even as part of a live audience—as different as being *in* a war, or a football game, or a hurricane is different from watching it on a movie screen. I can't get *inside* my body rhythm, because I can't find it, and therefore I can't dance. I was the only one out of fifty students who flunked a dance course. I remember the instructor telling me "You just have to *fall into* the dance", which sounded great; but I couldn't fall into the dance as I can fall into the music and get out of myself and become part of the music not only while singing it but sometimes even while hearing it.

As good music gives me "the good shivers" (*frisson,* holy fear, awe), bad music gives me "the bad shivers", especially those profoundly shallow "praise choruses" that confuse their infantile emotionality with sanctity. They make me feel excruciatingly embarrassed, as if I were watching a nudist colony of drunk Neanderthals loudly "sharing their feelings" about their feelings. Yes, I know the people who sing them are sincere. They are *terribly* sincere. So is Ned Flanders.

And so are the personal, spontaneous prayers of Evangelicals, which are precious to God. But they are not liturgy, and when they are said in public, like the preacher's required "long prayer" during the Sunday service, or my uncle's long graces before (ever-cooling) meals, I suspect that the words are directed more at our ears than God's. The word "show" comes unfortunately to mind, as in giving "a show" or "showing off" or "show and tell". I can conceive of nothing more insincere than a public display of your sincerity, or less humble than a public protestation of your humility.

For the sake of the law of non-contradiction, even if not for the sake of God, private, personal prayers should be—well, private and personal. They are like the silly things lovers say in bed, not like the solemn proclamations of kings and queens on thrones. At least that's how it always seemed to me. Perhaps I am just too private a person. I don't want to wear my heart on my sleeve, to show others my tears of love and anger, longings and fears, pleasures and pains. Especially the negative half. It feels like stripping naked in the presence of strangers. Nakedness should be only for your spouse or your doctor, and spiritual nakedness should be only for your Supernatural Spouse and your Divine Doctor.

This is one reason (not the only one) why I loved and attended Catholic, Anglican, and Eastern Orthodox liturgies while at Calvin. I also attended Protestant services (they don't usually call them "liturgies"), which usually have better hymns and better sermons. I pray daily for reunion so that we can all be as cool and classy as Episcopalians and as hot and sassy as Pentecostals at the same time. But this means the Episcopalianizing of the Pentecostal, not the Pentecostalizing of the Episcopalian. As soon as I discovered the liturgical prayers of the Mass, I used them in my private prayers with gratitude and appreciation and "heart". But the reverse does not work: good private prayers do not make good liturgy, even though good liturgy makes good private prayers. And yet, private prayers are even more essential—to salvation!—than liturgy. But the either/or is wrong: a crucifix is the apotheosis of both.

One Sunday I was at the Wealthy Street Baptist Church and heard a very inspiring sermon. The church had no symbols in it at all—no crosses, no statues, no stained glass windows—but I felt the strong need of something outside myself that I could see or touch to get me out of myself and to mediate and symbolize and sacramentalize the God to Whom I wanted to give my whole self in love and adoration, in response to that great sermon. Scanning, I found one tiny gold cross at the top of the flagpole on the stage. The Baptists had unwittingly allowed this one Catholic spy into their Cromwellian army. I addressed all my faith, hope, and love to the One who hung on that cross for me. I could not do without that physical icon. I could not throw my subjective self away out into what seemed to my body and my senses only as space, objective emptiness. The hand that received mine had to be as physically real as my own. I knew He was in me, in my heart and soul, but it was more important that I was in Him. I did not surround Him, He surrounded me. It was like C. S. Lewis' realization, in his autobiography, that "it was more important that Heaven should exist than that I should go there."

Perhaps the great saints and spiritual masters can sanctify and master that emptiness, but I am not a great saint and spiritual master. I am a cripple, and I need a crutch to walk. Religion is indeed a crutch, as the atheists argue. And until the atheist confesses that he is a cripple, he will not be in the market for a crutch.

The incarnate physicality that is so typical of Catholic worship—all its use of the five bodily senses (even the smell of incense)—is all this stuff "unspiritual"? Are Protestants more "spiritual" than Catholics? Do they not know that no one is more purely spiritual than the Devil? The Devil hates God and the entire physical universe He created. How can we try to be more spiritual than God, who gave us not just His Spirit but also His Body for our salvation? These thoughts came to me even before I seriously considered swimming the Tiber.

It is because both our humanity and our salvation include the body, because our Savior not only had a body but saved us by His body, that Catholicism adds a bodily, physical dimension to Evangelicalism. Tom Howard wrote a great book (actually, he wrote nothing but great books) entitled *Evangelical Is Not Enough*. Evangelicalism is necessary but not sufficient. It is the foundation but not the whole building.

And that physical dimension is not an *addition* to the essence but as essential as the spiritual. Christ saved us not merely or even mainly by giving us His mind, as all the great saints, sages, and philosophers did, but by giving us His Body. I intuitively knew and felt this "Catholic thing" even before I ever considered becoming a Catholic.

8

My First Explicit Step on the Road to Rome

My heart started moving down the road to Rome earlier than my head. It began with Saint Patrick's Cathedral and with my reading of Saint John of the Cross as a teenager, not understanding what he was writing about but "just knowing" that it was true, and real, and massive, like a mountain. But the first explicit intellectual doubt that perhaps we Calvinists were wrong and the Catholics were right about something specific came on my very first day on campus at Calvin.

My new roommate, Bill Brown, loved to argue (and so did I), and one of his questions sparked a debate among a few of us that lasted late into the night after supper that first day in the dorm. (We were not like today's students: we were actually more interested in exploring the truth right now than in making piles of money after we graduated.) Bill's question was: "Why don't we pray to saints, like the Catholics do?"

"Because we're not Catholics; we're Protestants", I replied.

"So we're Protestants because we don't pray to saints, and we don't pray to saints because we're Protestants. Is that a logical argument?"

"No, that's arguing in a circle."

"So why don't we believe in praying to saints like they do?"

"Because it's wrong. We're right and they're wrong. That's the only honest reason for believing anything or for not believing it."

"I agree", said Bill. "But that only raises the question Why again. Why are they wrong to pray to saints?"

"Because we worship God alone, and we pray to God alone. Worshipping saints is idolatry."

"So they worship saints?"

"Yeah."

"Is that the same as praying to saints?"

"Yeah, I think so."

"Is praying the same as worshipping, then?"

"I think so."

"I think maybe not."

"Why not?"

"If I ask you to pray for me, is that idolatry? Is that worshipping you?"

"Of course not."

"So why is it idolatry to ask the saints to pray for us?"

"Oh. I guess it's not, then, if that's all they mean by praying to saints. Is it?"

"I don't know. Do you?"

"No, not really."

"So what's the thing to do when you don't know?"

"Find out."

"Then maybe we should find out, eh? Isn't that the logical conclusion?"

It was a relatively minor issue, and Bill was not seriously thinking of becoming a Catholic; he was just arguing for the sake of arguing. Or perhaps he had discovered Socrates before I had. But in any case, his question made me realize that I ought to listen more before I judged and spoke. And that one little issue and that one large lesson gradually led to a few other little things, and then some bigger things, and then some more, as one little loose stone can start an avalanche.

9

The Fundamental Question about the Church

An incident in Rev. Weidenaar's class in church history explains the fundamental reason for my conversion perhaps better than anything else. The reason is the historical fact that Jesus Christ established the Catholic Church and gave her His authority.

On the very first day of class, Dr. Weidenaar asked us to define the church. No one answered. "You will have conversations with Roman Catholics. How is their definition of the church different from ours?" Again, no one answered. He persisted. "They will ask you what church you belong to, and you will say 'The Christian Reformed Church', and they will ask you when and where it began, and you will say it broke away from the Reformed Church about a hundred years ago, and the Reformed Church was founded by John Calvin during the Protestant Reformation about five hundred years ago. And then they will say, 'Well, too bad for you; sorry to hear that. You're in the wrong church. Because I'm in the church founded by Jesus Christ two thousand years ago.' So what do you say to that?"

Again, no one had an answer. I had already begun to be deeply interested in the claims of the Catholic Church, so I said to myself, "That's exactly why I took this course: to answer that question." I wanted to discover I was in the right church, not the wrong one. I didn't want to become a Catholic. It was scary and foreign and weird. All my friends were Calvinists. At that time I still saw Catholicism as an alluring but dangerous temptation.

The professor repeated his question: "This is a course in church history. So what's the difference between our view of church history and the Catholic view? And how do we answer their argument that our church is only five hundred years old?" Finally the brightest kid in the class answered: "It's our church that goes back to Christ, not theirs." "Prove it", demanded the professor. "You can prove it from the Bible", said the smart kid. "In the Bible the church is just a little group of Christians, a fellowship of disciples, who met together for praise and prayer and worship after Jesus ascended into Heaven." "So what is the Catholic Church then?" "It's the world's biggest religious business! Big organization and big laws and big money and big clergy and big dogmas and big power and big authority."

The professor smiled and drew two pictures on the blackboard. The first was a picture of a little acorn and a big oak tree. The second was a picture of Noah's ark. "Is that oak tree the same being as that acorn? Did the acorn grow into an oak tree like a baby growing up into an adult?" "Yes, of course." "Well, that's how Catholics see their church. The church in the New Testament was its baby form, and the church today is its adult form, but they say it's the same church. And they say that Luther and Calvin broke off some of its branches five hundred years ago and planted new churches, but that you can't do that; you can't start a new church. They say that they're in the real church, the first one, the oldest one, the one that Jesus founded, and that we're not. Now what's wrong with that argument?"

No one answered. For a second time I thought, "That's exactly the question I'm here in this class to find the answer to!" The professor moved to the second picture. "That's Noah's ark, which is one of the Bible's images or analogies for the church." Then he drew some little round things underneath it that were sticking to its hull. "Who can tell me what those things are?" The student next to me said, "They look like barnacles." "Right", said the professor. "You're a fisherman, aren't you?" "Yes", he said, pleased with himself. "Well, here's the real story of church history. Jesus founded the church, and it sailed along for fifteen hundred years, and it gradually got more and more corrupt and compromised and full of extraneous doctrines and traditions that didn't come from the Bible but from paganism, from Greek philosophy or Roman law—like barnacles that come from outside the ship, from the water surrounding the ship. And those barnacles will eat the wood and eventually sink the boat if they're not cut off. So some of the sailors, like Luther and Calvin, said, 'It's time to scrape off those barnacles', and that's what they did. We're called Protestants, or protesters, because we agree with their protest against those pagan barnacles."

I was hooked. That's exactly what I wanted to believe to justify being a Protestant. I raised my hand. "Professor, are you saying that if my Catholic friend and I both went into a time machine and went back to the early church, before the barnacles came onto it, that I as a Protestant would be more at home in it than he would as a Catholic?" The professor looked at me with a tilted head: "That's a strange way of putting it—time machine—but the answer is Yes. That is exactly what you would find."

I smiled and resolved to do exactly that: to enter the time machine of history and read the Church Fathers to find that I was indeed in the right church, the one my Lord had founded: a Protestant church, not the Catholic church.

If you are a Catholic, you know the rest of the story. It's inevitable. Once the question was rightly posed, as it was, the answer was almost guaranteed. Not a single one of the many Catholic "barnacles" that we Protestants called mistakes and falsehoods and extraneous additions to the original church—like the primacy of the Bishop of Rome, and the Eucharist rather than the Bible as the center of weekly worship, and the Real Presence of Christ in the Eucharist, and the Mass as not just a great prayer but a real offering of Christ for our salvation, and devotion to the saints and to Mary, and her Immaculate Conception and sinlessness, and her Assumption into Heaven, and Purgatory, and Baptism as salvific, not just symbolic, and Apostolic Succession, and the authority of Apostolic Tradition—not one of these so-called barnacles or new doctrines that Protestants found offensive and un-biblical and protested against ever caused any protest or controversy or appeared as new, as extraneous, as "barnacles" for 1500 years. They all evolved gradually and organically, like an oak growing from an acorn or an adult from a baby. The growth was organic, from within, not mechanical or engineered from without, like a machine.

What blew me away most was the history of the Eucharist. No Christian in the world denied the Real Presence of Christ in the Eucharist until Berengar of Tours, around A.D. 1000; he was condemned as a heretic, and he repented and was re-admitted to the Church—the Church that had always taught what I thought was the most stupid and most scandalous idolatry: confusing a little piece of bread with God incarnate, confusing mere chemicals with the

Creator of chemicals. I had to believe that the Holy Spirit had fallen asleep for fifteen hundred years, beginning—beginning when? I discovered that it was right from the beginning! For Protestantism did indeed begin two thousand years ago in Palestine, as we Protestants claimed, but it was not where we thought it was. When Jesus taught the Catholic truth about the Eucharist, in John 6, most of his disciples protested and left him. They were the first Protestants.

I didn't know the theological arguments for and against each of the distinctively Catholic doctrines that the professor called "barnacles", including the doctrine about Christ's Real Presence in the Eucharist, but I knew one thing for sure: that I had to be in the church my Lord founded. And the historical evidence that that church was the Catholic Church, the evidence that its history was a seamless robe, an unbroken continuity, an Apostolic Succession, became stronger every day that I read more and more of its history. I didn't have to prove each of those teachings to be true by my own research and argument; I only had to prove the authority of the Church that taught them. I was Mother Church's baby, and my job was to trust my Mother and the food she put on my plate, however it tasted. That was not an abdication of reason. It's only reasonable to listen to reason when the reason comes from God! It was most importantly of all not all the other books I read about church history but my Bible that told me that Jesus said to His Apostles, "He who hears you, hears Me", and that they ordained successors (called "bishops", "elders", or "presbyters") to carry on that authority until the end of time.

As Newman said, a Protestant immersed in history will not be a Protestant for long. For history is not theory but fact, data. Christianity is an essentially historical religion. Its central claim is not an ideal or an idea, not a feeling or a program or a morality or a mysticism, but a historical fact: the Incarnation, Life, Teachings, Death, Resurrection, Ascension, and Second Coming of Jesus Christ. And He didn't leave us in the dark. He established a Church that her earliest creeds call one, holy, catholic (universal), and apostolic. Those are the "four marks of the Church"—the true Church, the Church He founded. Protestant churches have only one of those four marks. They may be holy and foster holiness, but they are not one but many (thirty thousand different "denominations" all of whom contradict each other!), not universal but particular and local, and, except for the "high Anglicans", they do not even *claim* apostolic succession and apostolic authority. (I assumed that both sides of the Great Schism of 1054 remained parts of the one Catholic Church, like the east and west wings of a house, or, better, of a bird.)

It would take me a long time to learn all the official teachings of this Church and to evaluate all the arguments for them. It would take a lifetime. The single, simple historical argument that I have summarized above did not take a lifetime. And if it was right, all the other arguments for all the other doctrines were right, too, because God does not make mistakes. This was not the end of my investigation, only the beginning. But it gave me a new "default position", which was the Catholic claim that her teachings were from Christ Himself, handed down (the meaning of "tradition") from Christ to His Apostles and from them to their successors. And this chain, this Sacred Apostolic Tradition, led—where? To me! Just as the Body of Christ, the one and the same Body that was offered on the Cross for my salvation, was offered to me in the Eucharist, so the teachings of Christ were offered to me in the Church, which was *also* called "the Body of Christ". That claim no longer had to be proved by checking out each doctrine myself and proving that it was true, or at least in continuity with both Scripture and history, before I accepted it, so that only after all these different Catholic dogmas were proved could I know that the Catholic Church had the authority of Christ. Rather, she taught these truths because she had the authority of Christ, who was Truth incarnate. In other words, the onus of proof was on the non-Catholic to refute the one deductive argument rather than on the Catholic to prove the many inductive arguments.

The non-Catholic will reply that there are many such refutations of Catholic dogmas, and that if even one of them works, if it can be shown that any one of the dogmas that Catholics claim are infallible and authoritative is in fact false, or contradictory to Scripture, or to any of the other so-called infallible dogmas, then the Catholic claim for infallibility and Christic authority falls, too. So what were some of these anti-Catholic arguments? Were they all misunderstandings and prejudices?

Part of me was hoping I could find some, because it would be traumatic to leave the faith of my church, my friends, and my family. Another part of me was hoping I would find none, because the

Catholic faith was increasingly looking beautiful and wise and holy to me. My motives were conflicted, like the swells from an incoming and outgoing tide pushing against each other; but my demand for truth and for Christ's own will to be done was absolute.

In the next chapter I shall try to identify my seven most important anti-Catholic prejudices or misunderstandings, the seven reasons that kept me away.

10

My Seven Most Important
Anti-Catholic Objections

Objection 1

The most important Protestant objection, I think, was that Catholics did not know the single most important truth about Christianity, namely, the answer to the question "What must I do to be saved?" (Acts 16:30); that Catholics, like the Pharisees, believed in "works-righteousness", believed that they worked their way into Heaven by a high enough "merit pile", a sufficient number of good deeds (but how many is sufficient?), by a passing grade on their moral report card, rather than personally trusting in Christ, who offered mercy and grace to us if only we were humble and honest enough to repent and believe. In other words, "justification by works" instead of "justification by faith".

There is, unfortunately, some truth to that accusation against Catholics (but not against Catholicism). I often ask my "Catholic" students at Boston College to answer questionnaires about themselves, and I sometimes include the question "If you died tonight and met God and He asked you why He should admit you into Heaven, what would you answer?" And well over nine out of ten begin with the word "I" ("I did my best", "I tried to practice Your principles", "I am a kind person", etc.). About half mention and appeal to God's mercy, but fewer than one in ten even mention Christ.

But these Catholics are not giving the answer that the Catholic Church gives; they are not giving the Catholic answer. And I certainly cannot decide to join or leave a church because of what its uneducated or heretical members think, but because of what *she* thinks, and teaches. One can judge a church, not by its heretics, but by its believers. I may prefer nice Nazis to dastardly democrats as personal friends, but that does not justify me in preferring Nazism to democracy.

This first and most central objection I had to Catholicism is so important that I need to tell how I answered it here, before I go on to the six other, less serious objections.

If Catholics have forgotten their "evangelical" dimension of the absolute centrality of Christ, we need to relearn it, and Evangelicals can remind us of it. I suspect that God will not allow the scandal of visible disunity to end until Evangelicals can find in the Catholic Church a home for themselves and their fundamental and biblical (and Catholic!) conviction. It is indeed true, as Evangelicals love to say, that "The Church's one foundation is Jesus Christ her Lord"; and that "you can't get Christ out of the Church as you can get orange juice out of an orange." But you *can* get the Church out of Christ because He is her Creator. And the absolute centrality of Christ is essential to Catholicism, too, as our two recent wise and saintly popes, John Paul and Benedict, made constantly clear. In becoming a Catholic, I have not diminished but increased my Christocentrism. As Jews who become Christians say they are now completed Jews, more Jewish than before, not less; so I say that as a Catholic I am a completed Evangelical.

Objection 2

Another anti-Catholic prejudice is, I think, even deeper: it is the suspicion of sacramentalism. During the Reformation, the differences about the sacraments, especially the Eucharist, divided Protestants among themselves more fiercely than the issue of faith and works divided Protestants from Catholics. Naturally, for sacraments themselves are much more concrete than the relationship between faith and works.

The Catholic doctrine was that the sacraments worked *ex opere operato*, that is, from without, objectively, as real causes of divine grace entering our souls, rather than from within, subjectively, as only symbols, expressions, reminders, or prompts to the faith and love on our part that were the real causes of our receiving divine grace. But this "objectivism" seemed to me like materialism, or mechanism, a kind of religious technology (spin the prayer wheel ten thousand times, and a soul will get a higher karma and a better reincarnation). It sounded something more like pagan, un-Christian idolatry and magic than anything holy. It seemed impersonal and mechanical. That a Catholic would go to Hell if he committed a mortal sin and got run over by a truck on the way to Confession, but go to Heaven if the truck swerved, seemed to me absurd. To claim that the baby successfully baptized at one o'clock was free from Original Sin and could go to Heaven if he died at two o'clock but that the baby whose two o'clock Baptism was interrupted by an earthquake that killed him could not, seemed ridiculous. Of course the theology does not entail that absurd corollary since God "himself is not bound by his sacraments" (*CCC* 1257). That the Eucharist was literally Christ Himself seemed the most ridiculous and idolatrous thing of all: worshipping wine and wheat as if they were God.

This is not just about believed theology but about lived religion; not just about *The* Faith but about *my* faith. I know I am weak. I fear failure and frustration and suffering and sorrow and pain and impotence. I collapse, I despair far too easily. I have a strong mind but a weak will and undisciplined emotions. By conviction I am an optimist, but by temperament I am a pessimist, a Puddleglum. I know that nothing less than God Himself, nothing less powerful, nothing less wise, and nothing less loving, nothing less divine, can save me from that which I am, from myself. No one can save me from myself except the God Who created and designed myself. And I can touch God only in Christ. If Christ is not God incarnate, God remains distant, like a lighthouse, rather than present, like a ship's pilot. No idea, however true, no argument, however unanswerable, no insight, however profound, has the power to save me—me, this concrete human individual with nerve endings all over my body and soul. No ism, not even "Catholicism" or "Evangelicalism" or even "Christocentrism" can save me. Only Christ Himself can save me. When the waves of fear and weakness threaten to drown me, nothing "works" except hearing and believing His words: "It is I, be not afraid." "IT IS I." The "it" is an "I". The providential order of the universe and of my life, the tremendous truth that "all things work together for good for those who love God" because God is in control and in love

with me—this abstract truth becomes concrete only in Christ, in His
Real Presence, whether felt or only believed. In every event of my
life, He is speaking to me—not just to "man", but to me—personally
and individually. He speaks my name: "Peter, IT IS I; be not afraid."
I must believe and trust and hope, not just in the objective truth of
those words, but in the objectively real personal presence of the One
who speaks them to me, right now, at each moment, especially in
my bleakest moments. If He speaks, but not to me, if His hand does
not touch mine, I cannot walk through this valley of the shadow of
death; if He does, I can, because He is "with me". "Withness" is the
word of salvation.

And nothing trains me better to believe in that withness, to trust
that personal presence, than what Brother Lawrence calls "the practice
of the presence of God"; and nothing trains me better in that than
by adoring Him in the Eucharist. Why? Because He is really there! It
could not possibly be more simple.

Objection 3

Anti-Catholic prejudice number three was the claim of the Catholic
Church, in radical distinction from all other major Christian bodies, to be the one single visible institution that brought the whole
and unvarnished truth of Christ to us, to teach with infallible divine
authority. That seemed to me to be the most idolatrous, arrogant,
wicked kind of false prophecy on earth: to claim "thus saith the Lord"
for merely human traditions, inventions, and opinions.

But I did not notice that there were three similarly radical claims
that I did believe: first, the claim of the God of Israel to be the one and
only true God; secondly, the claim of Christ to be that God incarnate;
and third, the claim that the Bible is His infallible, authoritative revelation. If these three claims were false, they were also the worst kind
of narrowness and exclusivism and arrogance, not an innocent error,
but the result of a pride that was almost Satanic. But I believed these
three claims. The one about God makes either theism or atheism not
merely a mistake but an insanity. If God does not exist, believers are
worshipping a cosmic Santa Claus; but if He does, atheists are deny-
ing the existence of their own Father. And the claim about Christ's

divinity was the famous "Lord, liar, or lunatic" argument that origi-
nated among the Church Fathers and was made famous by C. S. Lewis
and Josh McDowell, two great modern Christian apologists who happened to be Protestants. And the claim that the Bible was infallible (a
claim made by the Church, by the way!) was also idolatry, idolizing
a fallible book, a "paper Pope". So the presence of radical "either-or"
claims was not foreign to me. But the extension of such "all or nothing" claims to the Church and the Eucharist were.

Objection 4

I also had a bit of the pervasive Protestant prejudice against Catholic
devotion to Mary. The prejudice was thoughtless, as it usually is.
It was taken for granted, not argued, for it was dismissed as below
argument, as absurd. It was taken for granted that Catholics' devotion
to Mary got in the way of their devotion to Christ, even though in
fact Mary's whole job and Mary's whole love is to point to Christ,
not to herself, and to bring us to Christ as she brought Christ to us.
To call Mary an obstacle to Christ was like calling a telescope an
obstacle to seeing the stars.

If a Christian is one who accepts Christ, Mary was the first Christian, at the Annunciation; so Mary is the first Body of Christ, the first
Church. But as a Protestant I thought that both she and the Church
obscured the centrality of Christ, as the moon obscures the sun during
a solar eclipse. However, I discovered that Mary, like the Church,
made me more Christocentric, not less. For she was in fact the most
powerfully Christocentric person who ever lived, and her whole work,
like the Church's, is to evangelize—to bring Christ to us, as she did
two thousand years ago, and to bring us to Christ today. If the essence
of Protestantism is Christocentrism, Mary is the greatest Protestant
who ever lived. She is the "Seat of Wisdom" literally because Wisdom
incarnate sat on her lap as a baby. Mary was His chosen earthly throne.

I began to see this only when I started to *pray* to Mary in the
Rosary instead of just reading about her, thinking about her, and
arguing about her. Our heads are taught by our hearts, and our hearts
are taught by our hands. What we understand most deeply depends
on what we love, and what we love most deeply depends on what

we do. Touching the beads aids praying the words, and praying the words aids believing and loving The Word.

I suspect there was also an unconscious prejudice there, perhaps not against women as such, but against femininity, as there is today in radical "feminism" (whose name is a perfect example of what Hitler called "the Big Lie"). This prejudice, common to both the radical "feminist" Left and the chauvinist Right, is based on a confusion between passivity and active receptivity. Mary was "docile" to God, in her mind, her will, and her behavior; but docility is an active virtue: it means "teachable", and merely passive things like blackboards, papers, and screens are not teachable; only active human minds are. The receiver who catches the football is as active as the quarterback who throws it.

Nearly every Evangelical Protestant who "has swum the Tiber" says the same three things about the issue of Mary. The first is that Catholic devotion to Mary was the last and hardest obstacle for them to get over in becoming a Catholic. The second thing is that after being a Catholic for many years, they now see Mary and Marian devotion as one of the most natural, right and beautiful things about Catholicism. The third is that now, from their newly Catholic point of view, they are amazed and surprised at how strong their former prejudice was, and they can't really understand it any more. In the first stage, the beauty and orthodoxy of Catholic dogmas about and devotion to Mary were incomprehensible to them. In the second stage, this thing that was so incomprehensible and feared was in fact comprehended and loved, slowly but effectively, more by practice than by thought. In the third stage, what is incomprehensible to the Catholic convert is why as a Protestant that beauty had been so incomprensible to him and why that prejudice had been so strong.

Objection 5

A fifth prejudice, much more implicit and unconscious, may have been racial. For many traditional Protestants, at least in my youth and in my circles, Catholics were stereotyped as dark, dirty, poor, uneducated, lazy, lusty, crooked, over-emotional, unpredictable, materialistic, worldly, unspiritual, and untrustworthy—especially the Italians and Spaniards. That was seldom explicitly said but commonly assumed; a kind of scent, more "smelled" than seen. Our textbooks were written in England, not Italy or Spain. Our history books celebrated "the glorious revolution", Cromwell, the defeat of the Spanish armada, Elizabeth, and even the French Revolution, as if atheism were less threatening than Catholicism.

Objection 6

A sixth prejudice was that the history of the Catholic Church was largely the history of corruption and tyranny. The Borgia papacy, the Spanish Inquisition, the condemnation of Galileo, the burning of witches (which the Church never did), and the Crusades were interpreted as typical rather than atypical. The only Pre-Reformation saints Protestants appealed to were either early Church Fathers or Augustine (minus his many very Catholic passages), but hardly ever anyone between Augustine and Luther, not even Aquinas.

When my Protestant friends at Calvin discovered that I was thinking of becoming a Catholic, one of them gave me Boccaccio's *Decameron* to deter me. It was ten funny and cynical short stories, mainly about corruption among Catholics. One story, set during the infamous Borgia papacy, had exactly the opposite effect on me than the one intended. In it, the pious Bishop of Paris had a Jewish friend, Abraham, a businessman, and the two discussed theology in a friendly way. The bishop thought Abraham was on the verge of conversion. One autumn day, Abraham told the bishop that he was about to sail to Rome to live with the papal family and do business with the Vatican bank all winter and would not be back until spring. The bishop, knowing how notoriously corrupt Rome was at the time, replied, "I know you are considering conversion. Why not be baptized here and now, before you go to Rome? Things are clearer here, and kind of foggy down there."

Abraham said, "No, perhaps next year, but not now. As a practical Jewish businessman, my rule is to do your business before you take your pleasure."

Abraham left France unbaptized, and the bishop thought he had lost him, but when he returned in the spring he told the bishop he was ready for Baptism.

"Oh, so you didn't go to Rome?"

"I did."

"So you didn't live with the papal family?"

"Yes, I did."

"And you didn't do business with the Vatican bankers?"

"Yes, I did."

"And now you're ready to join the Church? I don't understand."

"Look, I'm no expert in theology, but I'm an expert in business, and one thing I'm certain of is that no merely earthly business that stupid and corrupt could possibly last fourteen weeks. That one has lasted fourteen centuries. It's clearly a miracle. I'm sold."

I thought that was a very valid argument. Like the pope's answer to Napoleon when Napoleon kidnapped the pope and told him, "I will destroy your Church." The pope laughed, and said, "If we haven't destroyed it for eighteen centuries, you won't either!"

Objection 7

Finally, a seventh prejudice was more peculiar to me: a prejudice against bigness, organizations, and even communal enterprises, and a defense of individualism (for, after all, it is individuals who are immortal, not organizations). I forgot that the Church is an organism, not an organization, and Christ is her Head, not her CEO. I found Kierkegaard a kindred soul, and still do, especially in his critique of conformity in *The Present Age* and of taken-for-granted, comfortable, collective religion in his *Attack upon Christendom*. But I discovered that many of the Catholic saints sound the same notes. And that Catholic social and political wisdom teaches both the principle of subsidiarity (that no larger organization should do what smaller ones can do as well) *and* the principle of the priority of the common good (the rightness of self-sacrifice for others, whether the others are two or two million).

I never shared the prejudice against contemplation and mysticism; in fact, its presence in Catholicism was a drawing point. Josef Pieper's classic *Leisure: the Basis of Culture* was like a manifesto to me.

ও ও ও

My not-typically-Calvinistic love of leisure and contemplation was, I think, both an asset and a liability to me personally, but God uses both our assets and our liabilities as ingredients in His omniscient and omnibenevolent plan for our lives. Since we are exploring my early anti-Catholic prejudices, I might include here also the liability (essentially, laziness) that accompanied the asset since it, too, was relevant to my conversion.

When I was baptized into the Church by the Dominicans at Yale in 1960, I seriously thought of a contemplative vocation to the Dominicans. I was respectful of other orders, but both the Franciscans and the Jesuits seemed too activist and practical for my temperament. On the other hand, the Trappists seemed too severe for me, though I loved Thomas Merton's *Seven Storey Mountain*. I am, alas, both bored by and inept at most kinds of physical work, more especially technology, and most especially the whole digital world, which seems to me to have no depth, color, music, or mystery, just puzzles and problems. After all, there is nothing in its wholly quantitative mind except combinations of its only two "values" of plus and minus, infinitely complexified. Digital categories find no holding place in my mind, and when they enter it, they quickly slip away like riders falling off a greased pig. I'm not bragging, I'm complaining, about my incompetence: it is a burden in a world that is increasingly digital, and I thank God I am old and ready to escape this alien world and go Home soon.

I think God has designed everyone to have both a special talent and a special handicap, to deter us from both despair and pride. My talent is all things analogical, and my handicap is all things digital. I "intuit" well but calculate badly, boringly, sloppily, and forgetfully. I "see" well but compute poorly. When I first read Shakespeare, I *intuitively* saw him as a Catholic, long before that position became respectable from scholarly research; and when I read Chesterton's masterpiece *Orthodoxy*, intuitively I saw the same Catholic "big picture" there and was surprised to discover that he wrote that book many years *before* he became a Catholic. I saw the plant in the seed.

Prejudices are mistaken intuitions. The word means literally prejudgments, judgments we unconsciously make before all the detailed evidence is in. We all have prejudices, and perhaps the most damaging of all is the prejudice that we don't have any. That's like being proud of your humility. There were also some pre-conversion prejudices that were *not* mistaken, that moved my mind toward, not away from, the truth of Catholicism, as an invisible tide moves a visible boat that floats on the bright surface of its dark waters. I loved formal, regal, poetic language and discovered it in liturgies and prayers of the Catholic tradition. I loved strong, clear statements that sounded like tall and heavy vertical columns thrust into the ground from the sky, rather than shallow brooks or flat, empty highways, and I discovered this in the creeds. I loved tradition, authority, obedience, and hierarchy more than self-realization and equality and freedom and democracy; and I found these in the spiritual life. I loved the vertical more than the horizontal; Gothic cathedrals more than ranch houses.

I believe both of these are good, but without the first, the second becomes trivial, because depth is more important than breadth, quality than quantity. And if we have the first, we can easily add the second, but not vice versa; we can't get quality out of quantity. If there is no hierarchy, what becomes of the paradoxical *reversal* of the hierarchy, where the poor are raised from the dunghill and the rich go away empty? And what becomes of love? Three things passionate lovers never desire for themselves are *equality* (lovers "look *up* to", admire, almost adore, each other; it is not lovers but friends who are equal, side by side), *freedom* (lovers want to be bound to each other, not free), and *rights* (when we talk about rights, we are not in love but in justice, which is the default position, the defensive position, the second best).

Applied to the Church, this instinctive set of preferences helped lead me to one of the fundamental rational arguments of Catholic apologetics: How could this distinctive thing, this great and glorious thing, this regal thing, be wicked if it produced such great saints? How could it be ugly if it created such miraculous cathedrals? How could it be stupid if it produced minds like Augustine and Aquinas?

And how could it be so *interesting* if it is only a reasonable compromise? God Himself is wild (look at His answer to Job!); why shouldn't His Church be also? The Church is not the Church of clichés and platitudes; it is the Church of paradoxes and surprises. It is a strangely shaped thing, like a key, and thus apparently irrational in many ways. But, then, a lock is also a strangely shaped thing, like life itself; and if the key fits the lock, the match between these two irrationalities is the supreme rationality. And it "works" to open the door, and nothing else does. Walker Percy, when asked, "Why are you a Catholic?", answered simply, "What else is there?" The future first pope said the same thing: John 6:66–68.

I saw the same "key and lock" pattern, the pattern of rationality being found in the comparison of two irrationalities, in the famous *aut deus aut homo malus* ("either God or a bad man") argument that justified Christ's claim to divinity. The argument is that if he is not divine, he is either the world's greatest liar, if he knew he was not divine, or the world's greatest lunatic, if he thought he was. There is no possibility of a reasonable compromise here. And this argument applied equally to the Church and to her Eucharist: if her claims were not true, they were the most stupid and blasphemous set of claims of any institution in the history of the world, and in that case the Catholic Church was not just one among many denominations but the Church of Hell incarnate, a false prophet claiming "thus saith the lord" for her own heresies and claiming infallibility for a set of idolatries and idiocies like worshipping a wafer of bread and a cup of wine as if it were God Himself.

And if the Church were wrong, she would be not only not infallible but not even sane. Then how could the Bible be infallible, since the Church was the efficient cause of the Bible? It is a historical fact that "the Church (the Evangelists and Apostles) wrote the New Testament". It is also a historical fact that the Church was the "formal cause" of the whole Bible, in defining its canon. How do we know which books are infallible divine revelation if the Church that defined that list of books is not only not infallible but idolatrous and a false prophet? How can a fallible cause produce an infallible effect?

These ideas all came to my consciousness fairly late, but I think they were subconsciously conditioned, fertilized, and watered by my early, pre-Catholic loves. "Late have I loved Thee", Augustine prayed, for his later love of Christ and the Church were there in seed form in his early loves, waiting to be watered by the same Divine Farmer who had planted the seeds.

My ADD helped here, I think. It made me impatient and easily bored, so that I loved short, sharp, strong, clear, and "impatient" arguments like those. And short sermons, like the one God preached in four words to Saint Catherine: "I'm God. You're not." And those of Christ, the least garrulous, least sesquipedalian preacher who ever spoke. No one else ever said more in fewer words. God Himself spoke only one Word, one "only begotten Son"; and The Word Himself spoke very few words. His words were like His Body: "Infinite riches in a little room". The concentration of a diamond. The hardest and yet also the most beautiful.

11

How the Right Philosophers Helped

Dr. Jellema, my philosophy teacher at Calvin, helped me to see and respect the Thomistic principle that divine grace does not rival or demean or bypass nature and human nature but perfects it. Six applications of this principle are (1) that predestination turns our free will on, not off; (2) that faith perfects rather than rejects reason; (3) that reason perfects the will, the appetites, and the emotions; (4) that *agape* perfects *eros*; (5) that parents perfect their children, teachers perfect their students, and rulers perfect their people; and all because (6) God perfects man.

As a budding philosopher, this was especially striking to me concerning reason, which is one of the meanings of the incredibly rich Greek word *logos* that Saint John uses for Christ. One of my tasks in Greek class was to translate into modern idiomatic English all one hundred or so of the short fragments of the pre-Socratic philosopher Heraclitus. (They fill about twelve ordinary-sized pages.) Heraclitus uses the term *logos* dozens of times, and I discovered that both the literary context and the philosophical context required me to use many different English words or phrases to communicate the many shades of his meaning in that one word—for instance, word, language, speech, communication, revelation, teaching, manifestation, sign, proof, demonstration, intelligence, intelligibility, reason, logic, thinking, thought, truth, knowledge, wisdom, understanding, form, formula, essence, nature, meaning, order, structure, substance, and being. (!) *Logos* was what all the classic Greek philosophers sought and what the Sophists and skeptics, both ancient and modern, despaired of finding.

And there it was in the most profound chapter in the Bible, John 1: "In the beginning was the Logos, and the Logos was with God, and the Logos was God.... And the Logos became flesh and dwelt among us." Christ was the Logos. So the object of faith and the object of reason were in fact identical. Of course faith and reason were not identical. They were two different paths, but they were paths up the same mountain of truth to the same light of the same sun, the sun of God who is eternally the Son of God and who in time became the Lamb of God to take away the sins of the world. Since the Logos is the meaning of all things and since the Logos is Christ, Christ is the meaning of all things.

I found that ontological identity of the object of faith and the object of reason, of religion and philosophy, in Augustine and, earlier, in Justin Martyr, the first Christian philosopher and the Church's patron saint of all philosophers. Justin was bold enough to call Socrates a Christian because he lived and died for the Logos, the truth. Of course Socrates could not have known or even imagined that the Logos could be a Person, but he knew it was not merely a thought, an abstraction. He knew it as "The Good", by which he meant both our supreme good and goodness itself. We Christians would identify the first of those two descriptions, viz. "our supreme good", as the Divine Person of Christ, the ultimate object of religious faith, and the second, "goodness itself", as the divine nature of Christ, the ultimate object of philosophical reason. Reason and faith are two paths up the mountain that meet at the summit. And at the summit we do not merely find, but are found, for the Logos is not an abstract idea but a concrete Person who is active and who was drawing us like a magnet to Himself. That was the meaning of our own activity, our search. As the old hymn says, "I sought the Lord, and afterward I knew / He moved my soul to seek Him, seeking me. / It was not I that found, O Savior true; / no, I was found by Thee." Augustine writes, "I would not have found you unless you had first found me." I said above that Socrates could not have known that, but who knows, really? The humble Christ often acts anonymously.

I was thrilled to find that the Logos sought by all the philosophers that I loved was also the God adored by all the saints I loved. The home of all the Platonic "Ideas" or "Forms" was Christ, who was both the Mind of God, the Light of God, the Sun of God, and also the Son of God. This identity healed the split between my heart and my head. My prayers met my thoughts, kissed, and got engaged to be married.

When I tried to explain this in my chapel speech at Calvin, I did not know that its effects on my audience would be fame, scandal, confusion, and controversy to be remembered even years later. "What? Socrates was a Christian? That's heresy." No it isn't; and it is the opinion of great saints like Saint Justin and Saint Augustine and Saint Thomas, and even many Reformers like Erasmus, who famously said, "Saint Socrates, pray for us", and many Protestants like Arthur Holmes, at Wheaton, who famously said, "All truth is God's truth."

What books helped me most?

Chesterton (*Orthodoxy*, *The Everlasting Man*, and *The Catholic Church and Conversion*), of course. And, indirectly, C.S. Lewis, who never became a Catholic but whose *Mere Christianity* was much closer to Catholicism than to Protestantism. And Frank Sheed, "the Catholic C.S. Lewis", especially his three volumes of apologetics for street preaching. And Rumble and Carty, whose three volumes of *Radio Replies* answered all my anti-Catholic objections simply and clearly. Finally, Ronald Knox, whose *The Belief of Catholics* most directly confronted me and most definitively moved me over the edge.

The philosophers who tempted me in various "away" directions, especially rationalism, were Plotinus, Descartes, Leibnitz, Hume, Hegel, and Heidegger. The one who tempted me in the opposite, anti-rational direction was Kierkegaard. The ones I could muster up the least sympathy for were Bacon, Comte, Dewey, Ayer, and Sartre—only because I had not yet heard of Derrida or Foucault. I thought of Nietzsche and Russell as profoundly wrong, but at least they were interesting.

I see now that it was the individual philosophers, the persons themselves that I met through their writings, rather than any of their arguments, that moved me the most. I knew them only by their writings, of course, not by personal friendship; but I could tell from their writings, I thought, who were trustable and who were not, who were in love with the truth itself and who were in love with their own ideology. Thus even among atheists, I respected Camus but not Sartre, Beckett but not Foucault, Voltaire but not Derrida. I found some of the hardest-to-read theists were passionately honest and trustable, especially Marcel and Von Hildebrand. Their winning *personal* "style" came through despite their "losing" *literary* style.

And of course Aquinas was utterly winsome both in the clarity of
his arguments and in the honesty of his mind, as was Augustine,
who added a rhetoric that was to philosophy what Palestrina was to
music. (One could continue this musical analogy, pairing Aquinas
with Bach, Pascal with Chopin, Leibnitz with Mozart, Hume with
Schoenberg, Kant with Handel, Hegel with Beethoven, Heidegger
with Tchaikovsky, Kierkegaard with Sibelius, Nietzsche with Wag-
ner, and Derrida with John Cage.)

12

The Theological Issues

An Outline

We can look at the past, the present, or the future. But the only way we can look at the past is by looking backward from the present, because we exist and live and act and look only in the present. We are of course older in the present than we were in the past, and "older" is by nature (though not by necessity) wiser. Augustine could never have written any part of the *Confessions* at the time he was living it. An ironic corollary of this principle is that only after death will we completely understand our life on earth as a unified whole. The book is whole only after it is finished. "Call no man happy [i.e., finished, perfected] until he is dead." Only after it has lost its efficient-cause reality can it have its full formal-cause reality. A life, like a book, is fully itself only when it is dead and past.

My life is far from over yet, I hope; but the part of my life that this book is about is. And I think I can understand it better now than I did then. Looking back on the time of my conversion sixty-six years later, I now see ten fundamental religious or theological issues that pointed me in the same direction, like the ten fingers of two hands all pointing to the same thing. The issues were the following.

1. Church history. The first and most determining issue was the historical facts of the Church, for she *is* a historical fact, not an idea. The historical data, in Scripture, tell us that her origin is Christ. I doubted the Church, but I never doubted Christ as both *The* Lord and *my* Lord, nor did I as a Protestant doubt the Bible. But what did the Bible say was the relation between Christ and the Church? Did He "found" her, "invent" her, "author-ize" her and give her "author-ity"? That was a simple question of fact: Christ was a fact,

and the Church was a fact; what was the relation between these two facts? The Bible answers with three analogies: that He is her Creator and Inventor; that He is her Head and she is His Body; and that He is her husband and she is His bride. All three analogies forced me to raise my view of the Church up farther, closer to Christ Himself, than my Protestantism allowed me to do.

This issue of our connection with the historical Christ through the Church was so primary to me that I shall devote a whole separate chapter to it (the next chapter, chap. 13).

2. The "umbrella" principle in theology, the general principle that overarches nearly all particular Protestant-versus-Catholic issues under it, was the relation between God and man, the supernatural and the natural, Nature and Grace. And the Catholic principle that I saw consistently followed by the Church, but not so much by Reformation Protestants, was the principle that grace perfects nature rather than rivaling it. I saw this principle everywhere in Catholicism but frequently forgotten or violated in Protestantism. That principle is so pervasive that it also needs a whole chapter, especially its application to the relation between faith and reason, which is chapter 14. I also wrote a whole chapter (chap. 17) in my *Handbook of Catholic Apologetics* to show that a distinctive Catholic doctrine or emphasis is the fulfillment of every "mere Christian" principle that Protestants also accept.

The third, fourth, and fifth issues (below) were the three fundamental principles of Luther: *sola scriptura*, *sola fide*, and *sola gratia* ("Scripture alone", not Scripture and Tradition; "faith alone", not faith and works; and "grace alone", not grace and free will). All three are dealt with more fully in chapter 15.

3. *Sola scriptura* was the logical premise from which all the Protestant objections to Catholicism derived: "We don't believe this or that Catholic thing because it's not in the Bible."

4. *Sola fide* opposed both the Catholic "marriage" or "synthesis" of faith and *reason* in theology and also the Catholic synthesis of faith and good *works* (the works of love) in soteriology, or the science of salvation.

5. *Sola gratia* ("grace alone"), at least in Luther and Calvin, entails the denial of human free will. In that case, salvation is not, like marriage, a two-partner cooperation, like a duet or a dance ("it takes two

to tango"), but, like art, done "solo". God alone is the artist; we are only His brushes.

6. The Eucharist: Is it the greatest piety or the greatest blasphemy?

7. The sacraments in general and how they work *ex opere operato* (objectively); and the Catholic "sacramental worldview" and its rejection of Gnosticism.

8. The saints: Were they our idols or our allies in our spiritual warfare?

9. Mary: Was the great honor we gave to her our greatest obstacle to our fidelity to Christ or our greatest aid?

10. Thomas Aquinas: Was he the greatest Christian thinker who ever lived or a thinly baptized pagan Greek rationalist?

I don't remember exactly in what chronological order these issues appeared to me when I began to think about them seriously, during my years at Calvin; but their logical order and the order of their priority or importance became clear quite early. That's the order I put them in here.

13

The Facts of History

The primary issue to me was one of simple fact, just as the primary issue of Christianity itself is one of simple fact: Is it, or is it not, a fact that Jesus was and is who He claimed to be, viz. the Son of God and thus divine? And is it a fact that He really literally rose from the dead, which no mere man can do? So here, in the issue of whether Catholicism was true or false, just as in the issue of whether Christianity itself was true or false, the primary question was the historical, factual question: Is it a historical fact that Christ established the Catholic Church? In other words: Is there an identity and a seamless web of continuity between the thing Christ founded in the New Testament and called His "Church", on the one hand, and the visible institution that exists today and calls herself the one true Church, the one holy Catholic (universal) and Apostolic Church, which is the only Church that has those four "marks of the true Church" that are thus listed in the Nicene Creed? If so, I had to accept it because I accepted Him. If not, not.

Put another, simpler way: Who were the heretics, Catholics or Protestants? "Heresy" means literally "choosing for oneself" as distinct from faithfully obeying and handing on your assigned mission. Who were the "new kids on the block", the Protestants or the Catholics? That was a factual, historical question, just as whether Jesus literally rose from the dead or not is a factual, historical question.

Rudolf Bultmann famously wrote that "if the bones of the dead Jesus were discovered in Palestine today, all the essentials of Christianity would remain unchanged." That is perhaps the most spectacularly blatant contradiction to the New Testament that has ever been written. Compare what Saint Paul says in 1 Corinthians 15:14, 17–19: "If Christ has not been raised, then our preaching [the Gospel, the 'good news'] is in vain and your faith is in vain.... If Christ has not been raised, your faith is futile and you are still in your sins. Then those also who have fallen asleep [died] in Christ have perished. If for this life only we have hoped in Christ, we are of all men most to be pitied." The question of whether Christ founded the Catholic Church is just as central and crucial and also just as historical and factual and literal as the question of whether Christ rose from the dead.

He said to His Apostles, "He who hears you hears me" (Lk 10:16). He did not say, "He who hears you *will* hear Me also", i.e., because you will be My missionaries and lead others to Me, but "He who hears you *hears* Me (present tense)", i.e., because My authority is in My Apostles. Did that authority continue when the Apostles died, or not? The word "Apostle" means literally "sent out", on a mission. Was that mission *and that authority* passed on to their successors whom the New Testament tells us they ordained by "the laying on of hands" as their successors and who were called "bishops", "presbyters", and "elders"? If so, is the Catholic Church that exists today that same institution or not?

If not, if Christ established a Protestant Church, which either suddenly or gradually became unfaithful and fat with innovations and by such serious compromises with paganism, with Greek rationalism and Roman legalism, that it had become not only lazy, corrupt, and arrogant but apostate, then I had to stay right here where I was, in the church that called itself, not "new", but "reformed", returned, deloused, debarnacled. I had to say, with Luther, "Here I stand." Because it was the Catholics who were the heretics, the barnacles, "the new kids on the block", not us. Was it Jesus or the popes who invented Catholicism? Was it Jesus or Luther who invented Protestantism?

The same question, put "backward", so to speak, was: Is the claim of the Catholic Church today to teach only what Christ revealed to His Apostles and what they taught to their successors down through the centuries—is that claim true? If so, I had better get into it, because it's Noah's ark and He's Noah; He built that ark, and all the new little spiffy yachts, however nice they are and however sincere their builders were, and even if their passengers can get to Heaven, they are not the thing He invented. But if this Catholic claim to be the one Ark built by Christ the new Noah is not true, then I had to resist the temptations to fall in love with things Catholic because they were barnacles on the ark, not leaves on the tree or grapes on the vine.

It was a choice between two opposite interpretations of church history. One asserted a break, a discontinuity, between the old (Protestant) church and the new (Catholic) church, a "hermeneutic (interpretation) of rupture". The other was a "hermeneutic of continuity". I now see that this was very similar to the argument going on in American and European Catholicism after Vatican II between the two different interpretations of Vatican II: the "hermeneutic of rupture" and the "hermeneutic of continuity". Both the radical Left and the radical Right believed in the hermeneutic of rupture. The Left despised everything before Vatican II's happy rupture with the past, and the Right despised everything after Vatican II's unhappy rupture with it.

However, all the popes, and all the saints, like Newman, believed in continuity, not rupture, both in theory and in practice, both in principle and in historical fact, both today and in every generation in Christian history.

Apostolic Succession guaranteed that continuity. Christianity is essentially conservative, i.e., "conserving", because our supreme authority is Jesus Christ, Who is "the same yesterday and today and for ever" (Heb 13:8), not a "go with the flow" Christ who follows the winds of fashion to keep "up to date". (As Chesterton says, "How can anything be 'up to date'? A date has no character", and "he who marries the spirit of the age will soon be a widower.") The substance, the essence, of the Church's dogmas cannot change; only their applications to different times, the particular conclusions deductively drawn from their general principles, and the language of their articulation can change, as did all the Creeds.

This is not a political issue. Most people today identify themselves as "conservatives" or "liberals" (or "progressives") politically; but the Church is not a political party and cannot be judged or understood as if she were. The "theological conservatism" (or, rather, fidelity) of the Church to Christ and today's political "conservatism" are not the same, and neither can be either deduced from the other or refuted by the other. Christ, Christianity, and the Church are all "apolitical" in the same way as truth is multilingual: not by ignoring particular political parties or languages, but by transcending them.

The simplest and clearest way to answer the question of whether the Catholic Church was the church Christ established or not seemed to me to be to use as our standard the four "marks of the (true) Church" defined by the Nicene Creed (which we Protestants also accepted). A basic principle of all logical argument is that in order to find something unknown or disagreed about, we must begin with something known or agreed about. Ergo, to find Christ's Church, look for the Church that is one, holy, catholic, and apostolic.

The clearest of these four signs, I thought, was the word "one". The empirical fact is that there is no such thing as "the Protestant church" but only "the Protestant churches" and no such thing as "the Catholic churches" but only "the Catholic Church". That empirical and historical fact should at least make the Catholic position the default position, if not deciding the issue all by itself. After all, the Church is the Bride of Christ, and Christ is not a polygamist.

And if the Protestant answer is that the one true church is "the church invisible" and not "the church visible", that is a form of the heresy of Gnosticism, or spiritualism. Christ did not found merely an invisible or spiritual church, any more than God established merely an invisible or spiritual Israel. The Church is the new Israel, the ful-filled Israel. And Christ did not save the world by saying "this is my mind" but by saying "this is My Body." Like Christ, the Church is visible. She has a body. She *is* a body. "The Word of life" is some-thing we touched with our bodies' hands and tasted with our bodies' mouths and saw with our body's eyes (1 Jn 1:1). As Christ is one, His Church is one because the Church is His Body. He is not a dis-embodied ghost. And He is not a monster with many bodies. One Head, one Body. He no more has many bodies than the Church has two Heads.

This is how I would formulate the issue today. When I was still "shopping", it was not that clear to me, but it was moving in that direction. And what *was* clear to me at the time was that in the Bible (our agreed authority), Saint Paul was adamant about the oneness of the Church. He had absolutely zero tolerance for a plurality of con-fessions (read 1 Corinthians 1!) and was adamantly insistent about all Christians being "of one mind" (Rom 15:6, 1 Cor 1:10, 2 Cor 13:11, Phil 1:27, 2:2, 4:2, 1 Pet 3:8; 4:1), which he calls "the mind of Christ" (1 Cor 2:16).

My discovery was not just that Christ established a Church; that was obvious from the Bible. My discovery was that she was faithful and continuous in her dogmas for two thousand years. Apostolic Succession is a historical fact, and the teachings of that succession of Apostles (bishops), under the unity of the successors of Saint Peter as defined in the creeds and the councils, never changed; they just grew. The Church did not suddenly become apostate with Justin or Constantine or Augustine or Charlemagne or Thomas. From the beginning, she was Catholic, sacramental, eucharistic, and authoritative.

If the Catholic Church today is full of so many heretical barnacles, why did no one in the world, no saint or sage or prophet, ever notice them and protest until Luther and Calvin? Why the suddenness of the many radical critiques of the Church after 1517? Did it take Luther's loud rhetoric to wake up the Holy Spirit? Why were there no large defections from the Church because of her teaching on the Eucharist before the Reformers, except for a few lone heretics like Berengar of Tours around 1000, who repented, and then the Cathars and Albigensians in the twelfth and thirteenth centuries, both of whom totally disappeared, and John Hus, who was executed without leaving a legacy? Why did half the Christian world follow Luther and not Berengar or Hus? Were his hymns that much better?

These thoughts came to me gradually but irresistibly, like the tide, the more I studied Church history. Rev. Weidenaar's first class sparked the question in the first place (see chapter 9), and then the rest of his course added to my admiration of the early Church, when we went through all the Trinitarian and Christological heresies of the first six centuries and saw the Church narrowly escaping one reasonable-sounding heresy after another, usually opposites. For instance, Arianism argued that if Jesus was fully human, he could not be fully divine at the same time, and Docetism argued that if He was fully divine, He could not be fully human at the same time. The Church got every detail right about this most super-rational dogma of all, the Trinity. An iota subscript was the difference between *homo-ousion* and *homoi-ousion*, and that made the difference between orthodoxy (that Christ had fully *human* being) and heresy (that He had *humanoid* being, human-like being). It was like a little rudder steering a gigantic ocean liner.

About the Trinity it is simply a historical fact that Scripture gave us only the data; the Church formulated the theology or "theory" that alone did full justice to all the data. The progress of theology was like the progress of science that way. God entrusted to the Church the correct definition of the two greatest and most apparently impossible mysteries of the Faith: the Trinity and the Incarnation. And we Reformation Protestants accepted it, without noticing that in doing so we were not setting ourselves up as judges of the Church and her Sacred Tradition but accepting her divinely instituted authority. How could a merely human, fallible authority perform such a miraculous feat of defining the two greatest mysteries in the world while avoiding dozens of reasonable errors about them? (Of course we can't define the essence of the infinite God, but we can define many things He is not, many tempting things we can confuse Him with. That's what all the heresies did.) The more I studied Church history the more I saw the logical oneness of two authorities that I had separated: on the one hand, the authority by which she asserted and we Protestants accepted her Trinitarian and Christological dogma and, on the other hand, the authority by which she also asserted all the Catholic dogmas that we rejected, like the Mass, and the Papacy, and Purgatory, Mary's Immaculate Conception and Assumption, Christ's Real Presence in the Eucharist, and the *ex opere operato* power of the sacraments—and the authority of the Church.

I was no theologian, but if I accepted the authority of the Church as divine, I did not have to figure out by my own reasoning every single teaching the Church gave me; all I had to do was to have good reason for trusting her, and then I could trustingly and obediently eat all the spinach she put on my plate. She is, after all, "Mother Church". I was her child, not her parent; her student, not her teacher or her judge or her editor. She was teaching me and grading me; I was not grading and teaching her. And the more I came to know her, the more I came to trust her.

That's usually a long process, and that's why conversion is usually a long process, not a sudden logical insight or argument (though it is expressed that way in apologetics). It is a matter of personal acquaintance with Mother; a matter of *kennen*, the "knowledge" of a person, not *wissen*, the knowledge of an idea or a thing. Religion was not *Wissenschaft* (expertise, science), it was *Kennenschaft*, to coin a term: a "getting to know you". Getting to know the Church is getting to know Christ, for the Church is His Body, not His business. I can't know a person's body without knowing the person, and I can't know the person without knowing his body. But I can know a CEO without knowing his business, and I can know his business without knowing its CEO.

Even the sins of individual Catholics counted for rather than against this respect for the Church; for despite all the sins of her members (all the way up: Judas Iscariot was a bishop and the Borgia popes were almost the Church's Mafia) and despite her practical mistakes (too slow to condemn slavery, fascism, and her own pedophile priests; the failure of the Crusades, punishing Galileo, the Spanish Inquisition), she never taught heresy, never justified her sins dogmatically. She often messed up her life, but she never messed up her dogmas. She continued to teach the truth and goodness and beauty of the Faith that she sometimes spectacularly failed to practice. There is no other institution in history like that. Certainly, not a single one of the tens of thousands of Protestant denominations was like that. Even the ones that avoided such spectacular sins did not avoid heresies. Even when they were unchangingly faithful in their behavior, they were not unchangingly faithful in their teachings.

So it seemed to me that the very facts that Protestants so reasonably and rightly say count against the Church really counted for her. What other institution has maintained its teachings so faithfully even when violating them so spectacularly? When popes had mistresses and orgies, they never relaxed the law forbidding adultery. When they became conspirators in murder, they never re-interpreted "Thou shalt not kill."

Think of the Pazzi conspiracy, observed by Machiavelli, when the Pazzi family, which bankrolled the papacy and got the Borgias elected, tried to murder "Lorenzo the Magnificent" in the cathedral on Easter Sunday at the very moment of the Consecration at the signal of the priest. After the congregation saw this, they captured the archbishop who organized the conspiracy together with his co-conspirator and threw the two of them out the high window with ropes around their necks, and cheered while the two hanged men bit into each other's flesh, while the crowd tore the limbs off the other conspirators. Insane! Demonic! Self-destructive. Yet not destroyed.

Whether the Church had spectacularly corrupt and wicked fifteenth-century popes or spectacularly wise and holy twentieth-century popes, it made no difference to the dogmas she taught. No matter how badly the Church lived her teachings, she never un-taught them. Even when her leaders murdered each other, she remained one and alive. Even when the teachers became unholy, the teachings remained holy. Even when she became provincial and fought civil wars with herself, she remained Catholic (universal) in her doctrine. Even when her bishops were apostates, she remained apostolic. It is indeed a miracle, only the second continuing visible miracle in history, the other being the surviving and thriving of God's chosen people, the Jews. They also have a spectacularly bad track record of apostasy, according to all their own prophets. But they are God's first family, and we are His second. Both of His families are notoriously "dysfunctional". But they're His.

Unconsciously, I had as a Protestant looked at the Church as if she were supposed to be a museum for saints. As a Catholic, I see her as a hospital for sinners. In that hospital, her patients often fight with her doctors and nurses. In fact, the Church is a psychiatric hospital for the criminally insane. And I discovered that I very much belonged in her.

ಾ ಾ ಾ

These thoughts and arguments about the Church were just that: thoughts and arguments. However true they were, what finally moved me to the choice to become a Catholic was not a thought or an argument or an interpretation of historical facts but a vision of the Church herself. This "vision" was not a miracle, just a gift of grace in my human nature, the intuitive and insightful and imaginative side of my brain, which has always been more trustworthy than my rational, calculating side. The vision was like a filmed triple exposure, or a palimpsest—three layers of an old manuscript, three visions of the Church, one written over the other.

The first one was the one that appears to the eyes: a "ship of fools", a human thing, a visible institution and community of human beings, a few of them impressively saintly, but all of them sinful and imperfect, most of them lazy and ordinary and selfish like myself, and some of them even venal and hypocritical. A bunch of dirty little donkeys who wished they were stallions worshipping mainly in barns that were pitiful attempts to imitate cathedrals (and many not even attempting to, and thus even more pitiful), and spending most of their time doing the work that the rest of the world could often do better: social services or visual and musical arts. The drama of the Mass was indeed beautiful, especially if you believed the theology behind it; but it was hardly Shakespeare, and usually done with less attention and comprehension on the part of its "audience" than that of kindergartners with ADD at an opera. That was the Church visible. She was composed of mainly old ladies and very few teenagers. She looked pretty pitiful and shabby.

But then there was the second layer. It was the Protestant version of "the Church invisible". It was not a visible institution, but simply all the people who were headed for Heaven, a number known to God alone. It was not only invisible but abstract, like a list of names.

Both of these visions, the Church visible and the Church invisible, I believed, were true. But they were separate in the Protestant vision, like bodies and souls in Plato, like faith and reason in Ockham, like faith and works in Luther, like matter and mind in Descartes, like subjective motives and objective deeds in Kant.

Then I saw a third layer where these two dimensions were not separate but together as a single Greater Thing. It was a concrete Thing. I saw this Thing in my mind one afternoon when I was alone in my apartment at Calvin, praying for God's help to choose rightly. This third vision of the Church was neither the physical set of appearances that I saw and heard every Sunday morning, nor was it the spiritual abstraction that I believed was the souls of the saved, nor was it simply those two things separate but juxtaposed. It was a Greater Thing. It was neither a set of appearances nor an idea; it was a real Thing, a Great Beast, a golden lion, a dragon, a formidable army spread out through time and space, consisting of men and women and angels and prayers and cathedrals and incense and high and holy music. It was big and it was beautiful and it was terrible, i.e., formidable. It was the Church described in the New Testament:

For you have not come to what may be touched, a blazing fire, and darkness, and gloom, and a tempest, and the sound of a trumpet, and a voice whose words made the hearers entreat that no further messages be spoken to them. For they could not endure the order that was given,

"If even a beast touches the mountain, it shall be stoned." Indeed, so terrifying was the sight that Moses said, "I tremble with fear." But you have come to Mount Zion and to the city of the living God, the heavenly Jerusalem, and to innumerable angels in festal gathering, and to the assembly of the first-born who are enrolled in heaven, and to a judge who is God of all, and to the spirits of just men made perfect, and to Jesus, the mediator of a new covenant, and to the sprinkled blood that speaks more graciously than the blood of Abel.

See that you do not refuse him who is speaking. For if they did not escape when they refused him who warned them on earth, much less shall we escape if we reject him who warns from heaven. His voice then shook the earth; but now he has promised, "Yet once more I will shake not only the earth but also the heaven." This phrase, "Yet once more," indicates the removal of what is shaken, as of what has been made, in order that what cannot be shaken may remain. Therefore let us be grateful for receiving a kingdom that cannot be shaken, and thus let us offer to God acceptable worship [the Mass! *That's* why they built cathedrals.], with reverence and awe; for our God is a consuming fire. (Heb 12:18–29)

I saw it in my imagination as Noah's ark, which is the icon of the Church, her sacred symbol. It was concrete and visible. It looked exactly like it does in traditional Christian art, big and broad and high and wooden. On board were all the saints, as well as all the sinners. I did not ask how so many people could fit onto one little boat, nor where all the animals were, because I understood that this was an icon, a symbol; but it was a symbol that was real and true, not conceptual and invented. It was not a thing made out of the acts of the human mind, any more than it was made out of the atoms of wood and other matter that constituted the created universe. The atoms that made this single Thing were persons, both human (many millions) and angelic (many more) and divine (Three).

The Ark was the Church, and the sea it sailed on was time and history. It was like a Gothic cathedral in that it was not just one among many parts of the cosmos but a sacred symbol of the whole cosmos. It was also like a Gothic cathedral in that it looked like a rocket ship, its flying buttresses looking suspiciously like a rocket ship on its launching pad, ready to carry us spiritual astronauts into Heaven. It had gargoyles in it because it had everything in it. It was a microcosm, it was everything, it was "catholic", i.e., universal. For it was the Body of the Logos Who designed the whole universe.

Out of the central window of this Ark I seemed to see two figures who were looking at me, reaching out to me, and speaking to me. They were Augustine and Aquinas, my two favorite saints and the two greatest Christian minds of all time. They were inviting me to come out of my little lifeboat and let myself be hauled aboard the Ark.

So I did.

14

Nature and Grace

I gradually discovered, by induction from many examples, the universal theological principle that seemed to be the basis for nearly all the Catholic differences from Protestantism, namely, that the relation in human life and experience between nature and grace, or the natural and the supernatural, although it is a real distinction, is not a distinction between two separate realities. It is not an either/or, and not even merely a transcendence of one over the other (although it was that, too) but always an alliance, a marriage, a fulfillment, a perfecting. "Grace perfects nature." This is ultimately because God is love, and love always seeks the perfection of the beloved, and all that God created is beloved by Him.

Eschatologically, this means that if x is in Heaven, it will be perfect x, more x, than x was on earth, whether this x is a halo or a hamburger, a cathedral or a cat. Not more *than* x but more *x*, more "x-y". And x includes sex, in a transformed form that we cannot imagine and therefore should not try to. The "new heavens and new earth" will not lack anything good that was in the old one. God alone is all-sufficient, of course (if not, then God is not God but just *a* god), but God's glory will be reflected in finite creatures more, never less, there and then than it is here and now.

God is not competitive. Creatures can be competitive with each other, but the Creator cannot be competitive with His creatures. More than that, God wants to *marry* His human creatures, us, the ones He created in His own image, *persons*. Christianity, the gospel, is a marriage proposal. God is a marriage maker, not a divorce lawyer or a court judge.

There is a good theological and philosophical reason for this: God is not *a* being, like Zeus, but Being Itself, so He cannot be in competition with other beings. He is not one among many.

"Grace perfects nature." What does this mean in particular? Many
    things.
God perfects (and divinizes) Man.
The intellect perfects (and interprets) the senses.
Faith perfects (instructs and corrects) reason.
The will perfects (and orders) the passions.
The soul perfects (and gives life to) the body.
Light perfects (and makes visible) colors.
Man perfects (tames and humanizes) animals, as God tames and
    divinizes man.
Saints perfect (inspire, teach, and pray for) sinners.
Hope perfects (and justifies) optimism.
Supernatural charity perfects (and strengthens) natural friendship.
Love perfects romance (and turns it into fidelity and commitment).
Persons perfect things (by making them personal property).
Poetry perfects (and beautifies) language.
Music perfects sound (as form perfects matter and actuality perfects
    potentiality).
Marriage perfects (and is the teleology of) sexuality.
Predestination perfects (uses, actualizes, turns on) free will.
Supernatural miracles perfect nature (as space travel perfects our
    appreciation of earth).

It means, as Augustine strongly taught and as Aquinas reiterated and
as many early modern so-called Thomists denied, that there is in our
human nature a demand, a desire, a need, a relativity to grace; a "natural desire for God", in fact for nothing less than the Beatific Vision,
the participation in divine life itself, *theosis*. Although the fulfillment
of this desire can only be by grace, the desire itself, and its need, and
that design in human nature, from the beginning, even before the
Fall, is not itself a grace but a created aspect of our nature. We have
a natural objective need and a natural subjective (but usually implicit
or subconscious) desire for the supernatural. "Thou hast made us for
Thyself, and our hearts are restless until they rest in Thee."
    For me, as a philosophy major, the most important application
of this principle that grace affirms, perfects, and fulfills nature rather
than substituting for it or bypassing it was the marriage between faith
in supernatural divine revelation and knowledge by natural reason,

which was the fundamental enterprise of mainline medieval philosophy, most superlatively done in Saint Thomas Aquinas.

The identity of Christ with the *Logos*, the truth and meaning and wisdom that was sought by all the great philosophers, justified the marriage of faith and reason. For although the content of what is known by reason and what is known by faith are not identical (they overlap: some truths known by faith cannot be discovered, understood, or proved by reason, and some can; and many truths known by reason are no part of religious faith, but some are), yet there is an ontological identity between Jesus Christ, the eternal Son of God, and the Truth sought by the natural reason of the philosophers. Luther and Calvin divorced these two things that the medievals married. Luther went so far as to call human reason "the Devil's whore". If Luther and Calvin affirmed that the Logos was Christ, they did not affirm that Christ was the Logos, that He was the fulfillment of pagan philosophy just as he was the fulfillment of Jewish prophecy. They revived Tertullian's heresy "What concord hath Athens with Jerusalem?"

I call it a heresy because, in Vatican Council I, the Church affirmed, as an article of faith, that truths like the existence, oneness, and perfection of God were not merely articles of faith but knowable by human reason. What an ironic example of faith perfecting and justifying reason! It required faith to teach our reason that it does not require faith to teach our reason.

The Protestant tendency, almost "the Protestant principle", and the usual Protestant practice has been protest, negation, polemic, rejection (of things Catholic), seeing the twenty dualisms or doubles above as either/ors rather than both/ands, promoting divorce rather than marriage.

All these examples of the relation between grace and nature are important, but the most practically important one is one that biblical Protestants affirm as strongly as Catholics do: that the supernatural "Thy will be done" perfects my own will; that sanctity perfects human happiness; that dying (to oneself) perfects life; and even that suffering, accepted in faith, perfects joy. For the ego is not perfected by egotism; we gain ourselves only by losing ourselves, we find ourselves only by forgetting ourselves, and we obtain our true selves only by giving ourselves away. Every religion in the world knows some aspect of this great paradox: that to try to save your life and your self is to lose it, and to lose your life by giving it away is to save it. The supreme practical and personal instance of the principle that grace perfects nature is that self-sacrifice and suffering perfect joy. Only lovers sing.

And Evangelical Protestants certainly knew this, too, like the martyr-missionary Jim Eliot, explaining why he risked his life, and eventually lost it, by going to preach to the violent Auca tribe in Ecuador. He replied to his friends who called him a fool for such a risky venture: "He is no fool who gives up what he cannot long keep in exchange for what he cannot ever lose." Taoism also knows this principle well, for at the very heart of that religion is the Tao, "The Way", which is essentially this way of gain by loss; to be like water, seeking the humblest, lowest places in order to feed and give life to every plant, conforming to its container, serving rather than ruling. Islam knows it, too, for "islam" means total surrender to the will of the one God. Even Buddhism knows it even though it denies the substantial reality of both God and the soul. It knows that the abolition of egotism, of *tanha* or grasping, results in peace and clarity and "bliss", not struggle and confusion and pain. Its practice is admirable, however inadequate its theory.

This moral and practical dimension of the paradox, common to both Protestants and Catholics, is more personally demanding than any of the philosophical and theological and "theoretical" dimensions of it; for changing one's thought is not nearly as painful and difficult as changing one's life. So I, as a typically immature, childish, selfish, shallow, and sinful teenager, did not practice that principle very deliberately, and therefore I did not understand many aspects of the "theoretical" principle, either: since I did not suffer for it, I did not see that it solved the problem of suffering and explained the joy of Purgatory. I did not have what Newman called "real assent" to it as distinct from "notional assent". Only later did I come to understand the lesson that was practiced as well as taught by all the Catholic saints. I had admired the self-sacrificial saints, but from a safe distance. Life's livings teach more powerfully than Thought's thoughts. Works—the works of love—teach more deeply than faith alone.

Connected with this pervasive Catholic principle of grace perfecting nature, I discovered three related principles, which are really three other forms of it, or other aspects of it, or other ways of stating the same single principle: (1) the principle of "first and second things";

(2) the principle of the firstness of what Christ called "the first and greatest commandment" (and, negatively, the firstness of idolatry as the first and most universal sin); and (3) the principle of what Augustine calls the two freedoms, the higher freedom of liberation being the end and purpose of the lower freedom of choice.

1. The principle of "first and second things" is explicitly taught by C. S. Lewis in an article by that title. Because goods are in a relationship that is hierarchical, some goods ("first things") being higher than others ("second things"), therefore to sacrifice a "first thing" for a "second thing" is to miss not only the "first thing" but the "second thing" as well. For instance, to politicize art, as both Fascists and Communists did, is to destroy both art (a "first thing") and politics (a "second thing"). (If you question the priority of art over politics, ask yourself this question: Do you really experience more deep and heartfelt joy from good laws or from great music?) Another clear example: to neglect your family for your career is to mess up not only your family but also your career. To idolize a "second thing" is always to pervert it. Alcoholics cannot appreciate the divine design of alcohol: "to gladden the heart of man" (Ps 104:15). To reduce religion to social service, to prefer human things to divine things, is not only to lose divine things but also to mess up human things.

2. For second things, when put first, become idols, false gods. And that is why the first commandment is first: because all sin is a kind of idolatry, whether the idol is a demon, a drug, a statue, or an ideology; a thing or a feeling or even a human being. Thus the first principle ("first and second things") implies the second principle (the "first and greatest commandment").

3. And the second principle implies the third one, the one about freedom: that the purpose of the lower freedom, the freedom of choice, or freedom from determinism, is the higher freedom, the freedom of liberty, which is freedom from sin. For sin is separation from God, who is the Source of all goods, and therefore from every good, including the good of the lower freedom. Idolizing freedom of choice is like idolizing power; what is meant to be a good servant becomes a bad master. It seems to get you want you want, but it actually does the opposite. Thus the glutton loses his appreciation of fine food, and the moneygrubber loses the enjoyment of the things money can buy in worshipping money itself. The opposite of freedom is addiction, and both the sex addict and the i-phone addict lose the very pleasure

and power they seek. If we are addicted to our own pleasure, we find misery; if we are addicted to our own power, we find impotence; if we are addicted to our own contentment, we find discontent; if we are addicted to our health, we worry ourselves sick: hypochondria. The second thing, idolized, betrays not only the first thing but also itself. Only when put second is it perfected and fulfilled.

And these are all instances of the general principle that divine grace perfects human nature, as, within human nature, the soul perfects the body, and, within the soul, reason perfects the passions, and, within the body, the brain perfects the other organs. Thus Augustine says that God is to the soul what the soul is to the body.

And I learned that this was a clue, a pointing hand with many fingers, an "advertisement" and argument for Catholicism. For in almost all times, places, and cultures in our history, Catholics have understood this principle more clearly and consistently than Protestants; that is why they have produced such superior art, literature, philosophy, music, architecture, science, and politics. And human happiness. That is why *Babette's Feast* is a deeply Catholic movie.

I know of at least twenty people who converted from Calvinism to Catholicism. I do not know one who converted from Catholicism to Calvinism. Why exchange an aircraft carrier for a patrol boat?

Modern Puritanism drew many sincere Christians away from Protestant denominations, especially the Church of England and "mainline" American denominations, but very few from the Catholic Church. There were many purifying movements and reforming movements in the Catholic Church throughout her long history, including the Counter-Reformation; but until Luther and Calvin, none of them deemed it necessary to violate the Nicene Creed and sacrifice three of the four marks of the true Church for the other one: to sacrifice oneness, universality, and apostolicity for holiness.

This does not prevent Protestants from being holy. Indeed, many of them are saints. But except for Baptism, they lack valid sacraments, which are the Church's most powerful means to holiness. How ironic that their love of Christ coexists with their rejection of the Real Presence.

15

Luther's Three "Solas"

Sola Scriptura, Sola Fide, Sola Gratia

Luther thought of his three *sola* principles as his strongest theological reasons for believing that the Church had succumbed to non-Christian heresies. Here is how I came to see that they were in fact both his logically weakest and his most un-biblical points of all.

Sola Scriptura

This is the principle from which all other Protestant arguments against Catholicism are deduced. Protestants believe that Catholics believe too many things as divine revelation, things that are not in the Bible. Only the Bible has divine authority, say Protestants, not the Church.

I see a number of problems with this principle.

First, if only Scripture had divine authority and was infallible, then we can be certain only of Scripture. But this doctrine itself, viz. *sola scriptura*, is not in Scripture! So it contradicts itself.

It's like when I give my students assignments from the Bible, I say, "If you don't have a Bible, steal one." Abbie Hoffman, the rebellious hippie with a sense of humor, wrote a book entitled *Steal This Book*. My students get the joke. Steal the book that says "Thou shalt not steal." But Protestants don't get the similar joke: "Believe only what's in this book"—but that principle is not in that book.

And it is self-contradictory not just logically but also personally and religiously and practically, and it undercuts all our certainty in religion. Only God is self-certifying. We can trust Christ only because

He is divine, and we can trust His Church only because she is His, and we can trust the Bible only because it is hers.

To put the point simply, the Church invented the Bible, which is the book that tells us that the Bible did not invent the Church; Christ did.

Sola scriptura violates the principle of causality. The effect cannot exceed the cause. The Church invented the Bible, which is the book that tells us that the Bible did not invent the Church; Christ did. How can a fallible cause (which is what the Church is in Protestantism) cause (write) an infallible effect (the Bible)? How can anything give a perfection that it does not have?

That principle of causality, that the effect cannot exceed its cause, works for other Catholic things besides the Bible. How could a corrupt church produce so many saints? How could an ugly church produce so much beauty? How could a false church invent so many profound truths (truths even by Protestant standards)?

This was not a "knock-them-down-drag-them-out" argument to me, like the argument about the internal self-contradiction of *sola scriptura*; but it was data, it was relevant, it was there.

Another logical argument assumes Aristotle's common sense definition of the four meanings of "cause": the formal cause is the essence or definition; the material cause is the stuff or contents that the effect is made from, or made of; the efficient cause is the maker; and the final cause is the direction or design or end or goal or purpose. The argument above was about Scripture's efficient cause, which was the Church. The argument here is about its material cause, its contents, and its formal cause, its definition. How can a fallible definer infallibly define the canon of Scripture? How can we know what books are in it? Its table of contents was given to us, not by the Bible, but by the Church.

In other words, how can we trust the canon (list of books that are infallible divine revelation) if we can't trust the canonizer, the Church that told us what the canon was? The Bible does not come with its own Table of Contents. How do we know the Book of Revelation belongs in the canon? How do we know that the Gospel of Thomas or the Gospel of Judas doesn't? The only answer is that the Church tells us. But if we can't trust the Church that defined the canon, we don't know for sure what the canon is. And if we don't know what the canon is, how can we trust as infallible anything in it? If the canon is fallible, not only does the *sola* in *sola scriptura* fall, but so does the *scriptura* itself. Maybe Jesus didn't really say and do all the things our fallible canon says He did. Maybe not all things work together for good for those who love God. Maybe Jesus didn't literally rise from the dead. Maybe he never claimed to be divine. Maybe we don't even have God right because we don't have the canon right.

There is a single chain of causality here. If God falls, then the Son of God falls. "Like Father, like Son." If Christ, the Head of the Church and the "inventor" of the Church, falls, then the Church falls. "Like Head, like Body." And if the Church falls, then her authoritative Scriptures fall, the Scriptures she wrote and identified and authorized. "Like writer, like writing", "like author, like author-ity". And if the Church's authoritative Scriptures fall, there is no infallible divine revelation to judge our fallible human opinions, no divine standard to judge our human ideas.

Jesus can't be the infallible Son of God if there is no infallible God, and the Church can't be the infallible Body of Christ if there is no infallible Christ, and the Bible can't be the infallible Book of the Church if there is no infallible Church.

So my Protestant faith in Scripture rests on the authority of the Church. Which church? There was only one until 1517! That is a historical fact. Even 1054 was only a schism, not an apostasy; a separation, not a divorce. Catholics accept all the creeds, sacraments, authority, and scriptures of Orthodoxy, which has never split into thirty thousand denominations that contradict each other, as Protestantism has.

So in order to be a Bible-believing Protestant, I had to be a Church-believing Catholic!

Still another argument against *sola scriptura* is historical. It is the fact that nearly every Protestant denomination eventually, after only five hundred years, has done what the Catholic Church has never done for two thousand years, namely, changed her authoritative teachings to conform to changes in the culture, the *Zeitgeist* (the spirit of the times), or the latest theological fashion and popularity. Today, most mainline Protestant denominations have succumbed to "modernism" or "liberalism" in theology (skepticism of the supernatural and miracles) and morality (the Sexual Revolution). Nearly all have disobeyed Christ's own explicit words in all three synoptic Gospels in their saying yes to divorce even though He said no. In other words, they have claimed more authority than Catholics ever have, in contradicting and correcting the unambiguous words of a "hard saying" of Christ.

Even before I seriously thought of conversion, it bothered me that only the Church that seemed (to me as a Protestant) to put itself above the Bible has faithfully affirmed the authority and infallibility of the Bible in all things. The Protestant breakaways from the Church consequently lost the authority of the Bible: another example of the cause and effect principle. An infallible effect (the Bible) requires an infallible cause (the Church), and when the infallibility of the cause is denied, the infallibility of the effect necessarily falls, too.

So Protestants have succumbed to heresy not only by Catholic standards but even by Protestant, biblical standards. Nearly every denomination has contradicted the Bible as well as the Church at least on sexual morality, sodomy, marriage, and divorce, while the Church has never done that, despite two thousand years of temptations against every aspect of her teachings: Trinity, Incarnation, Church, sacraments, miracles, morality, or (today) sex. In two thousand years, she has never rejected any of her earlier infallible teachings, no matter how unpopular that "rigidity" and "narrowness" has seemed to others, and no matter how corrupt some of her teachers (bishops and even popes) have often been.

Saint Augustine famously wrote, "I would not believe the Bible if it were not for the testimony of the Church." The Bible itself calls the Church, not itself, "the pillar and bulwark of the truth" (1 Tim 3:15).

The logical validity of all these arguments against *sola scriptura* was decisive to my mind. But argument by itself did not move me to knock on the door of the Ark. It only disturbed the comfort of my seat on the little Protestant lifeboat I was sitting in. For Catholicism is more than the conclusion of an argument; it is a real Thing, and a big thing; and in order to embrace it, in order to marry it, we first have to see it as a whole big thing, like a person, and fall in love with it. You don't marry a person just because your logic proves that you ought to.

Perhaps the most impressive of the many arguments against *sola scriptura* is the fact that God entrusted the ultimate revelation, the ultimate mystery, the nature of ultimate Reality, namely, the dogma of the Trinity, not to the Bible, but to the Church. The Trinity, together with its corollary the divinity of Christ, is the most distinctively Christian dogma and the one that "goes all the way up" into the nature of God Himself. The *data* for the dogma are in Scripture: that God is one, that the Father is God, that the Son is God, that the Holy Spirit is God, and that the Father, the Son, and the Holy Spirit are three different Persons. But the creeds that accept and justify and correlate and explain all that data without ignoring or contradicting any of it—that is the work of the Church.

It is comparable to science. The data for Newtonian mechanics and for Einsteinian relativity are in the universe, but not the formulas. And none of the other scientists got the formulas right, as they did. Similarly, none of the other, heretical theologians got the formulas (the creeds) for the Trinity right. Only the Church did. Just as the history of science is littered with wrong theories about the universe, the history of theology is littered with wrong theories about God, broken trinities lying in the ditches beside the road of truth, while only the Catholic Church avoided them all and got it right, not only negatively (no heresies) but also positively (the creeds' many affirmations). She looks like Chesterton's famous image of the carriage wildly careening around corners and up mountain roads without barriers, avoiding all rocks and ditches and abysses, all the many heretical potholes and obstacles, each of which either sounded more reasonable or was supported by political and personal forces or both. Protestants cannot explain that fact.

And that fact constitutes a miracle. It is a historical fact that during the first six centuries, the Church, this "ship of fools" corrupted by fallenness of both mind and will, confusion, stupidity, laziness, pride, selfishness, arrogance, political machinations and personal ambitions, managed to get totally right the most difficult, unlikely, and incredible truth of all, the truth that defines the nature of Ultimate Reality. That is as unlikely to have happened without divine design as the genetic code randomly assembling itself.

Sola Fide

Sola fide seemed to me almost as weak a position as *sola scriptura*, and contradictory to many passages in Scripture. In fact, the Bible does directly, literally, and word for word give a simple and decisive answer to this question: Are we saved by faith alone (*sola fide*) or by faith plus the works of love? James 2:24 says: "You see that a man is justified by works and not by faith alone."

It could not possibly be made more stark and clear. Luther says we are justified by faith alone; the Catholic Church says we are not justified by faith alone, and the Bible says, word for word, that we are not justified by faith alone. Which of them agrees with the *scriptura* that Luther said was his *sola*?

When Saint Paul wrote that "the just shall live by faith" (Rom 1:17, KJV) he did not add the word "alone", and when he wrote that "we are justified by faith" (Rom 5:1), he did not add the word "alone". But when Luther "translated" that verse he *added* the word "alone" to Saint Paul's words. Which side is faithful to the *scriptura* that Luther said was his *sola*?

When Christ gave us his most extended parable about the Last Judgment, in Matthew 25:31–46, it was works, the works of love, that made the difference between salvation and damnation. Of course faith and works go together like a seed and a fruit, since one and the same thing, the divine life, *zoe*, supernatural life, comes into us by the door of faith and through us and out of us by the door of works. But that's the whole Catholic point: that "faith by itself, if it has no works, is dead" (Jas 2:17). Like the Dead Sea, which has an inlet (the Jordan River) but no outlet. (And equally dead are works without faith and hope, which is secular humanism.)

As soon as I met these arguments, in Catholic apologists, they seemed so clear and obvious that my previous strong conviction flew away like birds let out of a cage—the conviction that Luther had gotten right at least the most important thing, "What must I do to be saved?"

To affirm salvation by faith alone is to omit the most important thing of all, the most divine thing of all, the greatest thing in the world (1 Cor 13). The seed (faith) and the stem (hope) are there for the sake of the fruit or flower (love). And, as that great Protestant, Kierkegaard, says in his *Works of Love*, love, for Christians and for the New Testament, is not a feeling but a choice, a deed, an act: "*love is the works of love.*" That work is no more merely internal than it is merely external. It is an act of the whole person and, therefore, embodied, incarnated—like Christ.

And to admit, as Scripture clearly teaches, that the works of love are necessary for salvation, as the Church has always taught, is to eradicate the primary need for Luther's revolt, the claim that Catholics didn't know the most important thing of all, how to get to Heaven.

If Protestants reply that they accept this account of faith, hope, and love as three equally necessary parts of the plant that is our salvation, and if they interpret James 2, as Catholics do, in the "both/and" way rather than the "either/or" way, then both churches essentially agree about the answer to this most important of all questions, as was claimed by the "Decree on Justification" that was approved by both churches over twenty years ago. So where, then, is the need for Luther's revolt?

Justification by faith alone was, to Luther, and continues to be for most Evangelicals today, the central issue of the Protestant Reformation: the claim that Catholics didn't know how to get to Heaven, that they were guilty of legalism and "works-righteousness"; that they tried to merit Heaven by their good works. But the Church has always taught that no one can deserve or merit Heaven, because that truth is also repeatedly affirmed in Scripture—the Scripture that Catholics have always appealed to as their infallible data and standard and which they have understood as a whole, not by one isolated verse alone.

Sola Gratia

Sola gratia either means that salvation's cause is divine grace alone and not human free choice, as Calvin and Luther both taught, or it doesn't. If it does, that is both an anti-human heresy that lowers us to the level of brute instincts and an anti-God blasphemy that implicitly impugns God as arbitrary, unjust, and even cruel, for it implies that some go to Hell without freely choosing it, that God forces them there. And if it does not mean that, then why the need for the revolt?

Saint Augustine worked out the relationship between divine grace and human free will in two great books on the subject. He was a "both/and" Catholic who loved and affirmed and understood paradoxes. Nearly every heresy in history has selected one half of a paradox at the expense of the other: God's oneness and God's Threeness;

Christ's divinity and Christ's humanity; loving sinners and hating sins; justice and mercy; human ontological goodness and human moral badness; divine causality and human causality in sanctification; and divine grace and human free will.

Sola gratia denies the principle about nature and grace that I found universal in Catholicism: that grace does not rival, exclude, ignore, demean, or refute nature (and especially human nature and human free will) but perfects it, as Christ perfects the Law and as Christianity perfects Judaism. Thus a saint's choice to love God and man is more free, not less, than a sinner's choice not to. And it is more free because it allows divine grace to enter.

Divine grace is not merely power but truth (Ghandi: "God is not in strength but in truth"); and "the truth will make you free" (Jn 8:32). Animals have wills but not free wills because they are not *rational*. They can be "willful" but not free because they do not understand and cannot be motivated by truth. They can love food and sex but not truth and wisdom; they cannot be philosophers, lovers of wisdom. They cannot say, "I will choose to do this morally good deed because this is my moral obligation, and it is my obligation because it is the truth, because it is justice, which is simply the truth about right and wrong." Animals cannot understand "You must be holy because I the Lord your God am holy." The great "I AM" has no meaning to them. Animals can't be motivated from above, by truth, only from below, by instinct, passion, and desire, which are not free. Animals don't have free choice because they can't understand and be motivated by The Nature of Things, by Being Itself. Animals are not free because they can't do metaphysics.

And, as Aquinas so clearly argues, if there is no free will, then all moral language becomes meaningless: justice, charity, rewarding, punishing, counseling, and commanding. We don't do these things to even the highest animals or the most complex computers. We don't tell them to repent and go to Confession when they mess up. As Kant nicely summarizes it, " 'Ought' implies 'can'."

So grace-and-free-will is simply one example of the grace-and-nature problem, probably the most important one of all.

I knew that Catholics believed in free will, as Calvinists did not, and I thought this Catholic belief in free will demeaned the role of divine grace; that it made moral choices into a kind of 50-50 proposition,

thus limiting God's role in our lives, as if He carried one of my suit-
cases, and I carried the other one. I did not see how we could trust in
divine grace alone if we had 50 percent of the responsibility for what
we did, or even 1 percent.

I still remember a day of surprise and enlightenment at Calvin
College when I went to the library to check out for myself whether
our Protestant accusation of Catholicism as works-righteousness and
humanism was true or not by looking up what Saint Thomas Aquinas
said about the relationship between divine grace and human effort
in the "Treatise on Grace" in his *Summa* (I, 109). I found him asking
the following questions:

(1) Whether without grace man can know any truth? (2) Whether
man can wish or do any good without grace? (3) Whether by his own
natural powers and without grace man can love God above all things?
(4) Whether without grace and by his own natural powers man can ful-
fill the Commandments of the Law? (5) Whether man can merit everlasting life without grace? (6) Whether man himself and without the
external aid of grace can prepare himself for grace? (7) Whether man
can rise from sin without the help of grace? (8) Whether man without
grace can avoid sin? (9) Whether one who has already obtained grace
can, of himself and without further help of grace, do good and avoid
sin? (10) Whether man possessed of grace needs the help of grace in
order to persevere?

And the answer to each of these twelve questions was a resounding
"No." So much for the Calvinist objection.

So I discovered that the question dividing Calvinism from Catholicism was not whether man could do anything without grace, but
whether grace would do anything for man without man, without
using man's nature and free will as its instrument; whether the grace/
nature relationship was an "either/or" or a "both/and"; whether,
as Calvin saw it, the relationship between God and man, grace and
nature, was like the relationship between two creatures, one omnip-
otent and free and the other one weak and helpless, confronting each
other in a common field, a common world of activity; or, alterna-
tively, was it as Aquinas saw it, more like the relationship between an
author and his character, between Creator and creature, where the
Creator, Who was not *a* Being but Being Itself, Unlimited Existence
Itself, gave the creature his very existence and all his perfections and

by His grace perfected every aspect of it, including all his free acts. (The preceding complex sentence also, incidentally, shows why we should capitalize distinctively divine pronouns for the sake of clarity as well as piety.)

I discovered that, paradoxically, Calvin's concern to exalt the transcendence and "sovereignty" of God was done greater justice to by Aquinas than by Calvin. Aquinas, like Augustine, had preserved *both* the paradoxical "both/and" relationship between grace and nature *and* the absolute priority, transcendence, and sovereignty of God (*another* "both/and") better than Calvin had. Calvin's intentions may have been good and holy, but Aquinas was a better theologian because he was a better philosopher.

Yet the issue of how God's grace and our free will interact remained a mystery to me, and I suspect must always remain a mystery, like the Trinity and the two natures of Christ. However, since, as Aquinas says, we can know clearly and adequately what God is not, even though we cannot know clearly and adequately what God is, the refutation of heresies can be clear and certain, especially when they come in pairs that deny one or the other half of a paradox. And what can also be clearly and certainly known are the general principles that are relevant to that refutation, such as the reality of the data, of both halves of a divinely revealed paradox, even though not the relation between them, and also the principle that grace perfects nature.

But if grace and nature are allies, if grace turns free will on rather than off, why does God not give more grace to more people, so that all would make good choices and be saved in the end and no one would choose to rebel and be damned? And why does God give grace to this person and not that one at this time and not that time? Can God give more grace than He does, or not?

I know no positive answer to that question. I think it is impossible for us to imagine the relationship between God's will to save us and our will to resist Him. I think we will never have an adequate answer in this life to such questions that comes in a positive picture of the interaction between God's will and the will of an unbeliever on his way to Hell. And that's as it must be and should be. We are *meant* to live and think amidst fog and mystery. We are under the clouds, not over them. We are not God. How amazingly easy it is to forget that rather obvious fact!

Since we are not God and therefore our mind is not God's mind (Is 55:8–9), the most important thing we can know about what we can know about the answers to such questions is that we cannot know the answers to such questions. That was God's answer to Job, and it must remain His answer to us here under the clouds, until and unless He gives us a telepathy with His mind in Heaven. We need to get out of the play (human life on earth) and into the mind of the Playwright in order to see the play from His point of view. Meanwhile, the best we can do is to be faithful to the lines He has written for us—that is, to say, like Mary to His angel, "I am the handmaid of the Lord; be it done unto me according to your (revealed) word."

That, and not the greatest theology or even the greatest mystical experience, is our highest wisdom. And good Protestants and good Catholics can agree on that, at least, which is more important than all other agreements and the ultimate source and precondition for them.

16

The Five Points of Calvinism

The elucidation of mysteries is made significantly clearer (though never totally clear) from the refutations of heresies. So part of the answer to my question about the relation between divine grace and human free will is the falsehood of Calvin's heresy of "irresistible grace". This is one of the famous "five points of Calvinism" that are summarized in the popular acronym TULIP: "Total Depravity", "Unconditional Election", "Limited Atonement", "Irresistable Grace", and "Perseverance of the Saints". They are a "package deal", and they imply each other, at least in their simple and essential form, before we begin to make distinctions within each of them.

"Total Depravity" does not mean that we are as bad as we can possibly be or that there is no good of any kind in us in this world, even in those who are destined for damnation, but that we are totally helpless and incapable of helping ourselves to be saved or of freely cooperating in our salvation. It correctly asserts that without God we are absolutely hopeless, but it errs in deducing that therefore we have no free role in our salvation. For grace perfects nature.

"Unconditional Election" means that God first elects, or chooses, some and not others to be saved and then gives the grace of faith to those whom He predestined to be saved and not to those He predestined to be damned. He does not save us because we choose it, but we choose it because He has predestined us. The error of this Calvinist theology is that it puts God in time, in a before-and-after cause-and-effect relationship. Both Calvinism (which sees predestination as a prior cause and our faith as a consequent effect) and its enemy, Arminianism (which sees God as foreseeing our free choice and consequently saving us), commit this error, in opposite ways.

"Limited Atonement" means that Christ did not die for all men, to atone for all sins, but only for some, the "elect" or "predestined" ones. It directly contradicts Scripture, which repeatedly asserts the opposite, that Christ died for all men, or all mankind, or the whole world, not just for some (2 Pet 3:9). God's will for salvation is universal, but since we have free will (which Calvin denies), not all are saved, so God's will and God's grace are resisted to the end by some. So just as "limited atonement" implies "irresistible grace", so universal atonement implies resistible grace.

Grace is resistible. If it is not, there is no free will. And there is also a second logical argument for the heretical nature of the doctrine of "irresistible grace": grace makes us free, but forced freedom is a logical self-contradiction. Even God cannot do something self-contradictory because something self-contradictory is nothing. As Aquinas puts it, self-contradictions do not come under divine omnipotence. They are meaningless, and meaningless sets of words do not suddenly acquire meaning when you add to them the words "God's omnipotence can do this." So it is quite certain that damnation is possible, not because God wants anyone damned, but because although God's will is for all to be saved, and although God offers His gift of saving grace to all men, God's grace is resistible. It is a gift put into our hands, not a blow forced onto our skull; and the hands, unlike the skull, can open or close themselves. God is all love and grace, but He made His grace resistible by creating "resisters": us. And that gift of free will itself is a gift of grace. So it is grace that made grace resistible.

"Perseverance of the Saints (i.e., the saved)" may be true from the eternal, timeless, God's-eye point of view but not from the human point of view. It is empirically falsifiable. We observe not only unbelievers changing into believers (the Thief on the cross, e.g.) but also the opposite, people "losing" or rather rejecting their faith (e.g., Judas Iscariot). And what we observe is not an illusion. "Once saved, always saved" (the popular statement of this doctrine of "perseverance") is simply not true for us in time. It also contradicts free will and thus responsibility. If we cannot perform these two changes, from unbelief to belief or from belief to unbelief, then we are not free to choose. Worse, in that case God is responsible for our damnation as well as for our salvation—which is a terrible cavil and insult to God and a great danger to the heart of religion, which is the love of God for His goodness. To worship the God who wills to send some men to Hell is to worship what the Devil is, even if it intends to worship God and not the Devil. That (Mt 12:24–32) is a candidate for the unforgivable "deadly sin" (1 Jn 5:16).

I do not accuse Calvinists of worshipping the Devil, of course; but I accuse them of seeing one essential doctrine (the "sovereignty of God") as contradicting another one (human free will). Rather than being content with the paradox, like Augustine, with his typically pre-modern notion of reason and mystery as married rather than divorced, Calvinists embrace a modern concept of reason that does not begin by embracing and exploring mystery when dealing with dogmas. After all, the very word "dogma" served as an unfortunately one-sided English equivalent of what the Church Fathers called "mystery" (from the Greek *mysterion*). And a mystery, though it does not transcend the law of non-contradiction, transcends univocal, quantitative, digital, computer logic. "Either/or" does indeed correctly apply to propositions (they are either true or false) and to deductive arguments (they are either valid or invalid) but not to terms, especially to analogical terms, which have not just one but a range of meanings. Aristotelian logic has three "acts of the mind" and begins with terms, not with propositions, as the new logic does.

Thus Augustine, who uses the old logic, spends most of his time, in his two books on grace and free will, in contemplating and exploring the meaning of each of the two halves of the paradox (the two terms) before claiming to relate and reconcile them logically in the end. To oversimplify radically, "Grace" can come *to* us or *through* us (Christ the Logos being what Augustine calls our "interior teacher"). It can be either exterior (miraculous) or interior (providential). And "freedom" can be either freedom from determinism (free will, *liberum arbitrium*) or freedom from sin and its consequences (*libertas*). And even then, at the end of Augustine's book the resolution and reconciliation is only partial, as in a mystery, and not total, as in a problem. There is more light, but darkness remains also.

But those who follow Luther's and Calvin's nominalistic and quantitative "analytic" logic, the logic of Ockham, and, later, modern mathematical logic, cannot do this because for nominalism there are no real universals, no essences. To explore the mysteries of the Faith with that tool is like using an iPhone to do the work of an X-ray, or using a computer to do the work of a romantic lover.

All this is important, but it was peripheral rather than central to my conversion. For it was not primarily my disagreement with the "five points of Calvinism" that made me a Catholic. In fact *most* Protestants disagree with them, because most modern Protestants do not deny free will, as Calvin does; and even many Calvinists call themselves "two point" or "three point" or "four point" Calvinists instead of "five point" Calvinists, even though the five points seem to imply each other logically.

17

Sacraments, Sacramentalism, and the Eucharist

The three *sola* legs of the Lutheran tripod and the "five points of Calvinism" were both specific theological doctrines that could be argued about logically. But the Catholic "sacramental worldview", which was behind her teachings about the Mass, the Eucharist, and the sacraments in general, appeared to me as manifestations of a whole larger philosophical vision that could be approached and appreciated only by a "big picture" intelligence, a "seeing". It was like a work of art rather than like a theory in science. And therefore it took me a much longer time to "get" it. The same is true of Mariology: it is not just a theory in theological science but a masterpiece of divine art, and it usually takes time to "get" it, as it takes time to "get" why the Mona Lisa or the *Divine Comedy* is great.

Part of the problem of understanding both sacraments and Mary was a set of prejudices that I did not know I had. One of these was the "either/or" mentality: Mary *or* Jesus; body *or* soul, matter *or* spirit; nature *or* grace. My mind had two sides: a rationalistic, "either/or" side that loved arguments, syllogisms, and the scientific method, and also a "both/and" side that loved intuition, art, and contemplation. When I first learned the beauty and power of the syllogism, I conceived the project of putting all of philosophy into syllogistic form. (I was very inexperienced and naïve.)

Another prejudice was one that I took a long time to realize I had and thus a long time to overcome. This was an anthropology that was in fact, though not in intention, Gnostic, a "spiritual" view of "spirituality" that was suspicious of sacraments as something like spiritual machines, something "materialistic" and "magical" and superstitious. I did not recognize that I myself was a living sacrament, a holy material thing, not a soul haunting a body as a ghost haunts a house; and that my soul was not the only part of me that God valued for its own sake, since my body, as well as my soul, was created in "the image of God" (which Genesis 5:2 identifies as "male and female"!); that my body was not merely an instrument for my soul, as a car or computer is an instrument for my legs or my brain. It is not just a means but also an end.

I knew all this then and I now know that this instrumentalist or utilitarian view is also typically modern and accounts for our instrumentalization of persons, of sex, and of our own bodies. This de-sacramentalization and de-sanctification or de-secration of the body is one with the de-sacramentalization, de-sanctification, and de-secration of sex, which is the heart of the "sexual revolution" that is destroying our society, our safety, our sanctity, our sanity, and our souls. It is the new Gnosticism: the materialization and instrumentalization of the body and the spiritualization of the soul. Angels are spirits; we are not. We are embodied souls, or ensouled bodies. Souls, unlike spirits, are the souls of and for bodies. Our bodies are not merely complex physical machines, and our souls are not merely minds. We are "rational animals", not haunted houses. The "mind-body problem" is wrongly formulated; that is why no philosopher can solve it.

Although Gnosticism was known as a heresy as early as the first century (Saint John's first epistle targets it), it was pervasive in many Christian places and times. God raised up Saint Dominic and the Dominicans to refute it in its medieval form of Albigensianism (also Waldensianism and the Cathars). (Favorite Jesuit joke: What's the difference between the Jesuits and the Dominicans? Answer: Saint Dominic founded the Dominicans in the twelfth century to conquer the heresy of Albigensianism, while Saint Ignatius founded the Jesuits in the sixteenth century to conquer the heresy of Protestantism. Now tell me, how many Albigensians have you met lately?)

As a Protestant I did not "get" the Catholic sacramental worldview or even the Catholic sacramental view of men. That is why I thought of the Catholic doctrine that sacraments work *ex opere operato*, that is, objectively, from without, from themselves and their Divine Inventor, and not, like human art, only subjectively, from within, from our own spirit's faith and love, and dependent on and expressions of our subjective attitudes—I thought this was superstition, materialism, paganism, impersonalism, and mechanism, as if the sacraments were spiritual machines rather than personal works of God's art or, even better, acts of this love. I should have known that this made the sacraments very different than impersonal machines, since I knew that what we "get out of" an objective work of art, like a cathedral or a symphony, depends mainly on what we subjectively put into it, and therefore art and beauty vary subjectively very much, while a machine gives everyone the same infallible effect once we cause that effect by pushing a button or inserting an electric plug or a key. Even when I learned that Catholics were supposed to see sacraments as personal encounters with the person of God, as "I-Thou" relationships rather than "I-it" relationships, yet they still "felt" wrong—they were just too materialistic. (Gnosticism again!)

This was perhaps the longest and hardest prejudice for me to get over. I thought of Catholics as similar to Pharisees, who treated their external obedience to the minutiae of the Law in the same way as I thought Catholics treated receiving their sacraments, and both as similar to operating a complex computer.

I formulated my objection this way: I thought, How could it be true that if a baby died a second before the water of Baptism fell on his body, he would not go to Heaven because Original Sin had not been removed, while if he had lived a second longer, and received the "magic" water, he would? Imagine two sinners who were equally and sincerely penitent but only with "imperfect contrition" (fear of punishment). Both were on their way to the Sacrament of Confession. One was run over by a bus and died; the other got to Confession and died on his way home a few minutes later. How could it be fair that only the second would go to Heaven? Or, if both did go to Heaven, that the first person would need more Purgatory than he would have if he had made it to Confession, as the second person did? If two Christians, one Protestant and one Catholic, had the same amount of faith, hope, and love, and both received the bread and wine in "the Lord's Supper" how could it be fair that the Catholic would receive a grace that the Protestant could not receive? It seemed grossly unfair, materialistic, and both random and mechanical, more like our encounter with the universe than with a Person.

But then I realized a simple truth: that the universe is like that. Both subjective spirit and free choice and also objective matter and apparent chance make a difference to everything in our lives. We are not angels. One man is killed and another is not because of a quarter of an inch in the trajectory of a bullet. The woman who touched the hem of Jesus' garment was really healed, but if she had touched the hem of the garment of one of Jesus' disciples by mistake, sincerely thinking it was Jesus and having the same faith and hope and love as she had when she touched Jesus' hem, she would not have received His healing. How could this be? It's unfair.

But in that sense the whole world is "unfair" because we have bodies that are not simply instruments of our souls. Some are born with physical handicaps, others are not. Some get a terrible disease and others do not, even though both are equally careful and equally deserving. Job's three friends thought this could not be, that in a world subject to the Providence of a just God, all who suffer must deserve it, and therefore Job must be a great sinner. They were wrong, but their reasoning seemed right, because if they were wrong then it seemed to follow that God is either wicked or weak, either unwilling or unable to impose justice on the world.

So the issue is bigger than that of sacraments; the issue is that "Life is unfair." Aristotle and the Stoics both saw this when they taught that happiness depends on two things: the virtue and wisdom that are under our control and the chance or fortune that is not. When God finally answered Job's complaint that his life seemed unjust, He did not justify Himself rationally but pointed Job to monsters like Behemoth and Leviathan as God's own design for His Creation. God designed gargoyles as parts of His cathedral.

The only honest answer to the "problem of evil" is that human life is a very mysterious drama, and that our reason alone does not and cannot explain or justify everything in it. Only the reason, the *Logos*, of the Author who designed it, and not the characters in it, can understand it. We can only choose to trust the Author—or not. The heart, which loves it even when it seems irrational, has its reasons that the reason does not know. As Saint Thomas More said at the end of what is for me the greatest of all movies, *A Man for All Seasons*, when his daughter Elizabeth asked him how God could reasonably expect him to obey Him to the point of martyrdom, "Well, in the end it's not a matter of reason, it's a matter of love."

It took me a long time to come to that answer. In fact, most of its philosophical articulation came after my conversion, not before.

But the more specific problem, my reconciliation to sacramentalism, and to *ex opere operato*, and especially to the Eucharist, had to come before my conversion, or else the conversion would be dishonest. And for a long while I did not understand the Eucharist because I did not understand sacramentalism and the Catholic "sacramental worldview" in general.

However, I did not first come to understand "the sacramental world view" and then reconcile myself to the Eucharist, but vice versa. It was after I believed in Transubstantiation and the Real Presence and the efficacy of the Mass, on the authority of the Church rather than my own reasoning, that I understood sacramentalism in general. It was my love and trust in Christ that led me to love and trust the Church He designed for me; and it was my love of and trust in the Church that led me to love and trust His Real Presence in the Eucharist; and it was my love and trust of the Eucharist that led me to love and trust the Catholic sacramental worldview. In all three of these steps, it was love educating understanding. A love that was particular and personal educated my understanding of the whole general worldview of sacramentalism.

Why did I come to love the Real Presence rather than scorn it as an idolatrous heresy? Because it was obviously not a hateful and idolatrous heresy. So many wise and holy saints loved and believed it. It did not behave as idols behaved; exactly the opposite. "By their fruits you shall know them." The fruits here were immediate and interior, not just exterior: it was not merely that those who believed in the Real Presence loved their neighbors more (that was true, too, but not as easily seen), but that they clearly loved Christ more. Why? Because He was really there, right there in front of them, as totally and truly and literally there as He was on the roads of Palestine two thousand years ago. He was in them, too, but because of the Eucharist He was in their bodies as well as their souls. The body as well as the soul of Christ entered into our bodies as well as our souls! It enabled our love of Him to be focused and concrete, and love is always greater when focused and concrete than when unfocused and abstract. By loving Him, I learned to love, and by learning to love, I learned to understand and explain and justify my love. Saint Anselm famously said, "If you do not believe, you will not understand." This may not be true of mere intellectual belief, but it is true of personal trust and love. I came to understand that only later, after my conversion, which was largely, though not completely, intellectual.

Even before I understood Catholic sacramentalism, I found its presence throughout the Christian centuries, and I reasoned that it must be true if the Church taught it and the Church was authored and authorized by Christ. If not, if the Catholic dogmas about the Eucharist were false, then the Holy Spirit had slept on the job for fifteen hundred years, for every Christian in the world believed what the Church taught about it. So if the Protestants were right, every Christian in the world, including all the saints, had been victimized by the sorriest, stupidest, and most sacrilegious idolatry in history. There can be no *via media*, no compromise, about this, any more than there can be about God Himself (if He does not exist, He is the world's worst and biggest mistake) or about Christ (if He is not the Lord, he is the world's biggest liar or lunatic) or about the Church herself (if she is not Christ's infallible instrument, she is the worst and most arrogant false prophet ever, for no Protestant denomination ever made claims for themselves like the ones she did).

But didn't Luther and the high Anglicans also believe in the Real Presence? Yes, but they didn't *have* it because they broke Apostolic Succession. This connection between the two sacraments of the Eucharist and priestly Ordination made me realize that *ex opere operato* could not apply only to Baptism and the Eucharist but had to apply also to the Sacrament of Ordination, too, in order for priests to receive the power to consecrate the Eucharist. They received that power only through Apostolic Succession, i.e., from bishops who had been ordained by other bishops, and, thus, from the Apostles themselves, the first bishops and, thus, ultimately from Christ, Who authorized this chain of authorities, as we see in Scripture.

This need for Apostolic Succession for the sacraments to work *ex operato* also means that as a Protestant I could not be certain that my sins were forgiven, as Catholics could, because only Catholic priests have that authority, the authority to bind and to loose, to not forgive or to forgive sins, from Christ (again, as we read in Scripture), through Apostolic Succession (again, as we see down through all Christian history). As a Protestant when I sinned, repented, and sought forgiveness, I had to rely on myself, on my own sincerity and the perfection of my contrition. Coming into the Church liberated me from that same subjectivism that tortured and bedeviled Luther and led to his *sola gratia*—which *is* impersonal and mechanical because of his denial of free will. His *sola gratia* functioned as his substitute for *ex opere operato* in the sacraments. It was my belief in Christ's Real Presence in the Eucharist that most liberated me from that bedeviling subjectivism of Luther's, so that I could totally trust what was outside myself (Him, there) rather than what was inside me.

One day I realized that my objections to the "materialistic" Catholic doctrine of the Eucharist were objections to the Incarnation itself! A non-Christian could object to the Incarnation on exactly the same principle as a non-Catholic could object to the Eucharist. "How could you believe that what you see as bread is not bread at all but really Christ?" is similar to "How could you believe that what you see as a man is really God as well as man?"

I also learned that the Church had reasonable answers to the examples I had imagined against the Catholic teaching of *ex opere operato*— the examples of the baby dying one second before the water hit his head and the example of the bus-struck penitent on his way to Confession. Regarding Baptism, the Church's answer is that there are three kinds of Baptism, one ordinary and two extraordinary. The ordinary one is the Baptism of water. That's the front door of Heaven's mansion. There are two back doors for extraordinary situations. One is "the Baptism of blood", which is martyrdom. Those who died for Christ could not have missed Heaven just because they missed Baptism. The other is "the Baptism of desire": a sincere intention and desire, explicit or implicit, for Baptism can "count" as Baptism in such circumstances.

In the case of infant Baptism, the faith of the parents and the faith of the Church can put itself forward as a substitute for the baby, who cannot yet have his own faith. It is "their" baby, after all. They are not his owners or his employers or his creators, but they are his procreators, his parents. Both the Church and the family are organisms, not organizations. What else can justify infants being baptized before they can make a free choice? Baptists are quite consistent in rejecting both this Catholic vision of the Church as mystical, organic, and sacramental and also rejecting infant Baptism, for these two things are a "package deal".

The Church had wrestled with the problem of the eternal destination of unbaptized babies from the beginning and came up with a reasonable answer that never was either infallibly taught or rejected by the Church: that they went to Limbo, a kind of Heavenly kinder-garten. Since they had committed no actual sin that merited dam-nation, they could not go to Hell; but since they still had Original Sin, they could not enter Heaven. The idea of Limbo remains a theo-logical option (a *"theologoumenon"*, neither heretical nor dogmatic), but most faithful Catholic theologians today opine that God's surpassing love and cleverness will probably find "back doors to Heaven" for them. And that applies also to the mind-numbing millions upon mil-lions who have been murdered in their mothers' wombs, today's "holy innocents". For "where sin abounded, grace did much more abound" (Rom 5:20, KJV).

All seven sacraments come to us from the same authority, not from the Church, but through the Church from Christ. The Church did not write God's mail to us, she just delivers it. The Church can change any rule she makes on her own authority, e.g., rules about fasting or church attendance, but she cannot change any part of "the Deposit of Faith" she received from Christ. That is why she cannot ordain women or accept divorce and remarriage.

And regarding Confession, a sincere intention to confess can "count" as a Confession. God alone reads hearts. And of course, as the *Catechism* says, "God can also work outside His sacraments." For the man who was run over by a bus on the way to Confession, there is a non-sacramental "back door", namely, perfect contrition (which means the unselfish motive of doing the right thing for God's sake, not for the selfish motive of one's own escape from punishment). This is always available and forgives even mortal sins. One might perhaps call an imperfect contrition that sincerely desires perfect contrition a "Con-fession of desire" that can "count" just as "the Baptism of desire" does. For God sees the deepest desires of the heart and rewards them. He is never less than just, but he is also never just just; He is always more than just, in fact, more merciful and also more "tricky" and wise with His mercy than we can imagine.

So it is God's personality, God's love and wisdom and power, that explain the sacraments. Not only are they not impersonal and mechanical and materialistic, but they are at the farthest possible extreme from that. They are His kisses.

18

Mariology or Mariolatry?

Nearly all Evangelicals who become Catholics go through the same three stages I went through in their relationship to Mary.

The first, from within Protestantism, is the suspicion of idolatry; the perception that Catholics give more love and attention to her than to Christ. For most Evangelicals, this is not just one of many Catholic errors but often the most viscerally feared one of all.

Of course anything can be idolized, and all sins are in a real sense particular examples of the general principle of sins against the first and greatest commandment. But even if love and attention to Mary is excessive (which it isn't), that does not explain the passion of the Protestant reaction. Why is venerating a holy woman who was the Mother of God incarnate felt to be a worse example of excessive veneration than anything or anyone else, for instance, the bread and wine in the Eucharist, or the authority of the Church?

Something deeper and darker is going on here. The Devil seems to spend more energy persuading Protestants to stay away from Mary than from anything else Catholic. He clearly is terrified of her. Look what she did to his spectacular success in Aztec Mexico. (Read *Our Lady of Guadalupe and the Conquest of Darkness* by Warren H. Carroll. It is one of the most incredible true stories in history.)

It is no accident that radical feminists today, who hate, fear, and deny everything feminine, hate or fear or deny Mary. They envy the kind of power and strength that men have always excelled in, i.e., physical, external, aggressive, public, and political power; and they forget, ignore, deny, or hate their own superior power, the quiet, feminine power, the inner power, the spiritual power, the power of love and self-giving. And the power of giving life, which is the greatest power in the world, because it is a privileged image of the power that is divine, the power that holds the three Persons together in the Trinity. It takes far more power to make life or to give life than it takes to destroy it. Feminists often mock veneration of Mary as the veneration of her passivity, confusing humility and obedience with passivity, and not understanding the distinction between passivity (which is not alive) and receptivity, which is so alive and active that it "goes all the way up" into the Trinity: the Son and the Spirit are receptive, the first as eternally "begotten" and the second as eternally "proceeding" from the Father. Receptivity to God is not passive conformity and weakness, but the supreme source of life and power, creativity and activity; for the most active and powerful Person who ever lived on earth was also the most supremely receptive: He said He came into the world not to do His own will but to do the will of His father who sent Him (Jn 5:30) and that His teaching was not His own but His father's (Jn 7:16), yet He is equally divine (Jn 8:58). (Taoists understand that principle well. Even though they do not know God personally, they know His personality! Read the *Tao Te Ching*. It is almost the Sermon on the Mount.)

The Trinity is also the archetype and model for the family, which radical feminists also target, undermine, hate, fear, ignore, or even want to abolish, as Marx did. They reject the idea of both the father as the head and the mother as the heart of the family.

Radical "feminists" resent the objective fact that women are more receptive than men, both physically (the womb receives the phallus) and emotionally (women are more sensitive, empathetic, intuitive, personal, and relational). This fact of human nature was known to every culture in history until our own, which increasingly loves the unnatural and the "transgressive" and attacks the very idea of the natural and denies that we even have natures, especially sexual natures. This is an attack on order itself, on *Logos*, like Schoenberg's twelve-tone music, or Bauhaus architecture, or typically modern "art".

Mary is at the heart of the spiritual warfare that is destroying our Christophobic culture. She fights, but not as men fight. And as she conquered the old Aztecs, she will conquer the new Aztecs, who kill the same percentage of their children (one out of three) as the old Aztecs did.

Mary will defeat Satan totally in the end and will win the war for humanity. Satan probably knows this, and that is why he hates and fears her so much. She is "clothed with the sun" (Rev 12:1), which Satan fears (evil always fears the light of truth), while Satan is clothed with darkness, which she does not fear. Light always conquers darkness in the end. "The light shines in the darkness, and the darkness has not overcome it" (Jn 1:5).

The second stage of the Protestant convert's relation to Mary is a change of mind but not yet a change of heart, at least the intuitive and affective aspect of the heart as distinct from the deliberately willed aspect of the heart and its faith, hope, and love, which the convert already has. The Marian dogmas can be defended by good theological reasons, but the last obstacle that the Protestant has to overcome is usually not rational but irrational: his prejudices, misunderstandings, hesitations, and fears. And these surface more often in the Evangelical's aversion to the Church's Marian dogmas and devotions than in his aversion to anything else.

A convert usually does not convert to "cafeteria Catholicism", becoming a Catholic in some things but not others, so his second stage is to accept what the Church teaches about Mary because the Church has the authority of Christ and the succession of His Apostles. But the instinctive feeling is usually not fully there yet, with its telltale marks of positive joy, love, and enthusiasm. It takes the average Evangelical a long time to fall in love with Mary.

The third stage is the gradual falling in love, and that always goes together with a falling into seeing, into insight. The heat of love and the light of understanding go together like the heat and light of the sun. But there comes a time, usually years later, when the convert can honestly say that he no longer understands why he was so fearful of Marian dogma and devotion as a Protestant. He is not only freed from that fear but so radically freed from it that he cannot understand why he initially had it, why he found it so difficult to love and trust someone and something so beautiful.

In other words, at first he does not understand why Catholics are so in love with Mary, but when he does come to understand, he cannot understand why he at first did not understand. This was true in my case, too, and I think that it was not only my reading good Catholic books on the subject (Fulton Sheen's *The World's First Love* is my favorite) but also and above all my praying the Rosary that was the primary cause of this change in me, unconsciously. Before my conversion, I prayed the Rosary out of obedient faith and hope and love for the Church, but she taught me to trust, hope, and love Mary as more than an act of obedience.

It was similar to first accepting *Humanae Vitae* because it was authoritative and also reasonable, and then, later, reading John Paul II's *Theology of the Body* and adding the two precious dimensions of understanding it and loving it. In both cases, the progress consisted in joining my conscious and my unconscious mind. The unconscious mind is like the dark underwater swells and tides in the sea, and the conscious mind is like its surface waves that come to the light. The heart is like a sea made of blood, and when it pours its swells of blood into the brain, it is like the tides watering the tidepools of the land and enabling them to bring life into the light under the rays of the sun. Life comes from beneath; light comes from above.

The practical, psychological aspect of this analogy is in praying the Rosary my hands educated my heart and my heart educated my head. I think that's how it works not only with the Rosary but with many other things in life. Rationally, we like to think we should act, with the hands, in accordance with and in obedience to what we value, with the heart, and that we should value with the heart what we know to be true and good with the mind; and that is of course correct. But in life, the order is usually reversed. We learn by loving, and we love by living and doing.

But the mind was needed, too. The key doctrinal principle, the "big umbrella" principle that divine grace perfects human nature, helped me with the Church's Marian teachings. Because God was to her all that God could be to any human being, she was all to Him that a human being could be. It was all God's doing, but that meant that it was her doing, too. It was all grace, but Mary was absolutely "*full* of grace", as full as any merely human being ever was or could ever be. She was full of God incarnate in her body, as no one else was, and she was also full of Him and His love in her sinless soul. And that fullness was not something to be suspicious of as impossible, but something to exult in and even expect, as fitting, if indeed God was as generous with His grace as He was. And how generous was that? Always more generous than we imagine, hope, or expect. We should expect the unexpected from God. The exaltation of Mary's nature was the effect of the exaltation of His grace. And it

made Mary the most beautiful of all creatures, for the greatest of all
beauties is "the beauty of holiness" (Ps 96:9, KJV).

My typically Protestant suspicion was that, at least in practice if
not in belief, Catholics put Mary above Jesus and eclipsed the Divine
Son with the Marian moon. I now see that as not only a mistake but
a ridiculously absurd one, because no one is more Christocentric than
Mary. Her whole work is to "show unto us the blessed fruit of thy
womb, Jesus". She is indeed like the moon, but she reflects the light
of Christ the sun far more than all the other stars in the sky. And that
is because of her glorious receptivity. She gives herself totally, in body
and in soul, to Him. She almost disappears before Him in her humility, and that is why she appears so gloriously. That is why in Scripture
she does almost nothing else (for to bear God the Son is already everything) and says almost nothing else except her "Magnificat". And she
continues today to act, to intercede, to direct our attention to Him,
not to her, even though she is more worthy of our attention than any
other creature, even the greatest of the angels. I was afraid of Mary
because I wanted to be Christocentric, but she was the greatest of all
aids in making me Christocentric. No one ever loved Christ more,
and Christ never loved any creature more.

And He gave her as His last gift to us, from the Cross before He
died, when John was the only disciple who faithfully remained there
at the Cross. He stayed together with Mary more than all the others
did, and therefore he stayed together with Christ more than all the
others did. Christ's last command before He died was to John, and
thus to us: "Behold, your mother", and He said to Mary: "Behold,
your son", entrusting Mary to us and us to Mary (Jn 19:26–27).
Christ here told Mary to "behold" and care for His disciples, His
Church—us. Even when we forget her or reject her, she never for-
gets us or rejects us but mothers us with her powerful intercessory
prayers to her Son.

Mariology is the prime example of a pervasive difference between
Catholics and Protestants: that Protestants are essentially "protesters",
negative, fearful of error, critical of the many things they sincerely
believe make Catholicism too fat, too full of "barnacles", of additions
to Scripture. Their critique of Catholicism is that it is "too much".
And in itself, irrespective of its object, a negative critique is honorable
and necessary. All the prophets denounced sins and errors, especially

idolatry. But Catholics are also critics: their critique of Protestantism is that it is "too little", too skinny. Which is worse, believing too much or too little?

Just as Christians believe more than Jews do, so that Jews (and Muslims, too) see Christians as idolaters, believers in too much—too many persons in God, too many natures in Jesus—so Catholics believe more than Protestants do. It is, of course, not an absolutely universal principle that it is always right to believe more and never right to believe less, but is it not at least much more *likely* that the error is "too little" rather than "too much", if Shakespeare was right when his Hamlet told Horatio that there were "more things in heaven and earth", not less, "than are dreamed of in your philosophy"? Simple, pious people believe more than sophisticated, suspicious people, and they are usually right, at least about the most important things.

Mary is in one sense the greatest priest and in another sense not a priest at all. Women cannot be priests because they cannot represent Christ. They can do one half of what priests do but not the other half: they can represent mankind to God as well as men can, but they cannot represent God to man, because God appeared to us in Christ as a man, not a woman. This is simply an historical fact and not male chauvinism; in fact, it is almost female chauvinism, because to God all human souls are like women: brides, wombs, receivers (though active and free). But Mary performs the other half of the priesthood better than any man can. She most perfectly represents the Church, and thus all of mankind for the Church is the "Bride" of Christ.

The spiritual marriage between Christ and His Bride, the Church, the marriage of which all earthly marriage is an image (Eph 5:31–32), the marriage that is the end and consummation of human history (Rev 21:2), is not a homosexual marriage. It fulfills the God-designed human "image of God", which according to God's own Word is in sexual differentiation itself (Gen 1:27). Like the body itself, sexuality is not merely biological and not merely earthly.

At the heart of our culture war is not an overvaluing of sex but an undervaluing of it. It is at the heart of human nature, which is the image of God, and that is why what is at stake in this war is not just eight billion human beings but human nature itself. Satan cannot abolish God, so he is trying to abolish man. No mere man can stop him, but a mere woman can. Catholics know her name.

19

The Communion of Saints

Even before I ever had any thoughts about embracing Catholicism, I had an instinctive love of three distinctively Catholic things: the beauty of the liturgy and of cathedrals, angels, and the Catholic dogma of the "Communion of Saints". I did not understand that dogma when I was a Protestant, but I felt the pull. It is significant, I think, that if there was any one moment of decision for me, it was that moment at Calvin, alone in my room, when I sensed the greatness of the Church as a gigantic Noah's Ark with my two favorite saints, Augustine and Aquinas, on the deck waving to me and inviting me to come aboard.

I also remember my immediate, instinctive "yes" reaction to the incident I read in a Protestant preacher's autobiography when he recounted his father's death, when he was a young child. On the day of his father's death, as he had done every other night, he prayed for his father; but his mother, who overheard his prayers, corrected him: "We must not do that, son. We are not Catholics." The author said that he immediately felt as if a grill of iron had been lowered between him and his father by his mother's words, and he knew, with an assurance that needs no reasons, that she was wrong. Her words had separated him from his father even more severely than death itself had done. When I read that, I felt the same self-evident judgment about his mother's words: "This cannot be!" The Church militant, on earth, the Church suffering, in Purgatory, and the Church triumphant, in Heaven, is a single family, and we are never alone in any one of those three stages of our journey. Only if we go to Hell do we go "alone into the Alone". Plotinus, who wrote those famous words, was a great pagan mind and mystic, but he was as totally and disastrously wrong when he used those words to describe Heavenly experience as Sartre was when he said, in *No Exit*, that "Hell is other people."

I think it is also providentially significant that my very first conscious piece of reasoning about Catholic teachings, sparked by my roommate's question the first night I was in my Calvin dormitory, was about "Why don't we pray to saints?"

I also remember the *frisson* I felt when I first realized that the familiar verse in Hebrews 12, that we are "surrounded by so great a cloud of witnesses", meant that this cloud was not just past history but present reality ("we *are* surrounded"); that I was running a race in a great stadium and being seen and cheered on by my great heroes who were not past but present, who were watching me from their Heavenly seats. What difference does this make? The difference between playing alone in an empty stadium and playing before thousands of people who know us, love us, and are cheering us on. Imagine how you would feel if you saw them now—right now, thousands of faces looking and smiling at you.

And these "witnesses" ("witnesses" = "seers, those who see") are not only humans but also angels. If we saw right now what is in fact true at all times in our lives, namely, the fact that our guardian angel is totally aware of us, guiding us by many "subconscious" inspirations and guarding us against unimaginably great present dangers from the evil spirits who are formidable and much closer to us than we can imagine; and if we saw the myriads of other angels around and behind our guardian angel—what difference would it make? I suspect that we would not be able to endure that vision; that God mercifully and providentially tempers that north wind to the flesh of the shorn lamb in limiting what we see and feel. We are not yet great enough, and we must become great enough, to endure that vision.

And this is surely one of the reasons Purgatory is necessary for the vast majority of us: to give us the solar sunglasses that enable us to see the Heaven that surrounds us, to see the sun, who is the Son of God, without going blind. I think the greatest and most powerful sufferings of Purgatory come from the arrows of truth that break our heart, both the arrows of joy from the light of God and the arrows of sorrow from the darkness of our sins. Even now the little arrows that we experience, the arrows of both great sorrows and great joys, are more than we have room for in our souls, so that our souls *leak* both from great joy and great sorrow; and those salty tears are like the waves of the sea that escape their bounds when God's Spirit-breath blows on the waters and raises waves that flood our landlubbers' safe, dry lives, sweeping everything away in their path.

The sudden realization of the presentness of God, His saints, and His angels in the Mass and also in our ordinary purgatorial everyday sufferings was to me like my sudden realization that the confession at the very heart of Christianity was not that Jesus *rose*, but that He *is risen*. The tense of the verb is crucially important. He is not past and finished but present and active, "alive and kicking". Grammar counts. The words are exact: present tense, not past tense.

Similar was the realization that in the Eucharist He is not just "hidden" but "hiding", *latitas*, present tense, active verb, playing His holy hide-and-seek with us.

And, more generally but no less pungently, His last promise was not that He *will* be with us always but that "I AM with you always" (Mt 28:20). Present tense, not future. For He is God, and God is not "I was" or "I will be" but "I AM." And this eternal, timeless I AM is with us in our time, at every time. Perhaps it is better to call Him timely than timeless.

 ❧ ❧ ❧

The following "saint story" in my life occurred years later, but it naturally fits here. When I was in the long process of writing my novel *An Ocean Full of Angels*, I often went to Nahant, two tiny, beautiful islands connected to the mainland by a causeway ten miles north of Boston, because only there did I consistently get inspiration for the novel's plot, which had to evolve and change many times. In particular, I loved Bailey's Hill and its rocky beaches, where most of the novel's action takes place and where it is quite possible that the dead Viking at the center of my story (Thorwald Erikson) is buried. I brought Saint Kateri Tekakwitha into my story *before* I knew that the house I always parked in front of when I went to Nahant belonged to the mother of the boy born deaf whose miraculous healing, attributed to Saint Kateri, brought about her beatification. I also discovered in the Nahant library a painting by the boy's mother of Bailey's Hill with Thorwald Erikson and Kateri Tekakwitha together looking down over it from their Heavenly background!

Another "impossible coincidence": at a rectory in Chicago, I met a priest who had a huge collection of relics of canonized saints. He wanted to give me one, and he asked me if there was any one saint I was especially interested in. I replied, "Kateri Tekakwitha." He said, "I knew it. Hers is the only relic I have two of." I now have a first class relic of Saint Kateri. My wife was especially interested in her in college, and so were my daughter and my son-in-law, who is part Native American and who works at the Kateri shrine in Auriesville, New York, and whose daughter is named Kateri.

In a providential world, nothing is random, nothing is a coincidence.

20

Saint Thomas Aquinas

This will be a very short and inadequate chapter on a very large thinker, in both body and soul. I regard him as the most intelligent, clear, correct, complete, and comprehensive thinker who ever lived. Though a great saint, he was not the greatest saint who ever lived. That was Mary, and no one but God knows who was second—Mary Magdalen? John the Evangelist? John the Baptist? But being a saint is incomparably greater than being the greatest thinker. I took "Thomas" as my confirmation name for two reasons. One was because his providentially decreed vocation is mine, too: writing words, many words about philosophy and theology. The other was that he clearly knew that one Word is incomparably greater than all other words. Of the many stories about him, my favorite one is his three-word answer to Christ's question that He asked him from the crucifix shortly before his death. He had finished the part of the *Summa* about the Eucharist, and his confessor Brother Reginald swore that he heard Christ speak these words to Thomas from the crucifix: "You have written well of me, Thomas; what will you have as your reward?" And Thomas's reply was: "Nothing but Yourself, Lord."

It was the most perfect possible answer to the most important question in the world, the question of "the meaning of life", the object of our heart's deepest love. Jesus began his ministry with that question. Look it up in John's Gospel 1:38. His very first words were: "What do you seek?"

I think the second best thing Saint Thomas ever said was when he was explaining why he would write no more. Reviewing the millions of words that he had written (they were literally millions) and comparing them to the vision of Christ that he had seen directly in a mystical experience, he used a single word for what all of his words seemed to him to be, and why he could write no more. The word was "straw".

Straw was used in the Middle Ages to cover dung from horses, cows, and bulls. It is a shocking word, and similar to another S-word Saint Paul used in a similar context to summarize all his human achievements compared to knowing Christ: the Greek word *skubala*. Look it up in the old King James version, which here dares to be literal. It's in Philippians 3:8.

Saint Thomas married incomparably important pairs of goods better than anyone else, *ever*: grace and nature (see chap. 14), faith and reason, clarity and profundity, common sense and brilliant intelligence, the natural and the supernatural, intuition and reasoning, heart and head, openness and conviction, complexity and simplicity, the one and the many. He could say more in fewer words than any other philosopher. I have found reading Aquinas' *Summa Theologiae* to be more edifying to my prayer life than reading nearly anything else outside the Bible. (I anthologized and explained some of these *Summa* passages in *Practical Theology*. If you like them, read the rest of the *Summa*: it's only four thousand pages long.)

G. K. Chesterton, who never went to university but who wrote the best book ever written about Aquinas (there have been thousands), says that nearly every other system of philosophy contradicts common sense at some point, but Aquinas' never does. Perhaps that is why Thomas, like Aristotle, is the most ignored or despised philosopher in Western culture among most philosophers for the last five hundred years. (Hobbes is a prime example: he is positively allergic to Aquinas and to Aristotle, and even to syllogisms.)

Aquinas, I discovered, was deeply Protestant in every *positive* way as well as totally Catholic. He spent most of his life preaching Scripture. And therefore he strongly defended both free will and divine sovereignty, and the absolute priority of grace, as Augustine did. His theology is both Bibliocentric and Christocentric, for both Scripture and Christ are "the Word of God". The Bible is the Word of God on paper, and Christ is the Word of God on wood (the wood of the Cross).

I suspect Aquinas himself had a lot to do with my conversion. I hope that in Heaven there will be space for me on the long lines of people who want to thank him for having cast so much light into our foggy minds. He, Socrates, and Augustine have been my three main models for philosophizing, as Pascal, Chesterton, and C. S. Lewis have been my three main models for popularizing that philosophy.

I have spent the last eleven chapters on eleven ideas, eleven aspects of my conversion. All of them emerged while I was at Calvin. It is now time to return to the biographical facts. Once I was convinced, converted, and confirmed, what happened next?

21

Philosophy at Yale

I wanted to go to Oxford for graduate work, but Oxford required my having participated in college varsity sports, and the only varsity sport Calvin had was basketball, at which I was quite clumsily inept.

It was Dr. Jellema who recommended Yale to me and me to Yale. Yale's graduate school then had the most stringent entrance requirements of any in America. Jellema's recommendation must have gotten me in. His academic reputation was considerable even though he never published a book. (This was back in the "dark ages" when academia was more informal, personal, and relaxed, and before uniform professional regulations like "publish or perish" were invented.) He had taught at Indiana University and, according to a well-known rumor, had a standing offer to teach at Harvard, which he declined in order to serve his own people at Calvin. But when his body (but not his mind) got old, Calvin would not exempt him from their mandatory retirement age. Teaching was his life, so he taught at a public college (Grand Valley) for about ten more years.

When I arrived at Yale, I was surrounded by geniuses, on both sides of the teaching desk. Many were eccentrics, both among students and among professors.

My favorite teacher at Yale was Brand Blanshard, who was probably the most sheerly intelligent man I ever met. He was an atheist, a rationalist, and a Hegelian. His classic defense of Hegelian idealism, *The Nature of Thought*, ranks in my mind as only one step below Kant's *Critique of Pure Reason*, one step above Spinoza's *Ethics*, and two steps above Sartre's *Being and Nothingness* as one of the four most sheerly and formidably rational books of philosophy I have ever encountered. I deeply disagree with Kant's idealism, with Blanshard's Hegelianism even more, with Spinoza's pantheism even more, and with Sartre's nihilism most of all, but all are masterpieces of rational argument, and I cannot imagine myself refuting them by pure reason alone.

Blanshard was also one of the most totally polite, fair, open-minded, and intellectually charitable men I have ever met. He was always totally calm and reasonable and chose his words with the highest care and economy. He reminded me of Thomas Aquinas in his style, method, and personality, though he defended a philosophy that was in many ways at the opposite end of the philosophical universe from that of Aquinas. He gave me Highest Honors on my term paper defending the epistemology that he thought the least defensible of all, viz. the "naïve realism" or non-critical realism of Aristotle and Aquinas. He wrote on it: "This paper reminds me of 'The Charge of the Light Brigade': hopeless from the beginning in its chances for success but admirable in its courageous, clear, and forthright shots right into the face of the enemy."

In his popular and always-crowded epistemology seminar, I was, I think, the least brilliant of twenty-four brilliant students. The twenty-four of us were all in disagreement with Hegel and Blanshard at the beginning of the course, but by the end of the course his defenses against all of our arguments for all of our alternatives had won the day in the field of fair argument, even though not in the field of our personal conviction. I don't think any of us were personally converted to Hegelianism. We felt like almost all students when first exposed to Anselm's "ontological argument": unable to refute it yet unable to agree with it.

In his seminar, each of us had to present a defense of a controversial issue in epistemology, and I chose the issue I disagreed with him the most about, viz. the relation between reason and religious faith, and I defended the philosopher Blanshard confessed he had the least sympathy with personally, namely, Kierkegaard. He was so honest and gracious that he confessed his previous "take" on what he had called Kierkegaard's "simplistic fideism and fundamentalism" had been itself "somewhat simplistic, fideistic, and fundamentalistic". Though he was an adamant atheist, he admitted that Kierkegaard, as I had presented him, had a far more reasonable and justifiable basis for the "leap of faith" than he had realized.

His assignments in the epistemology course were the most demanding of any course I ever took: for each class we had to read and understand, without secondary sources, about one hundred pages of very abstract and high-level arguments from the greatest thinkers in history about the most abstract and difficult division of philosophy. I remember much mental exhaustion from that class. In comparison, most of the other professors at Yale were lenient almost to the point of laziness.

One of them was a famous scholar of Kierkegaard, but I walked out of his class after four or five sessions because, though charming and clever, he never got past what for Kierkegaard was the least valid of all "ways of existence", viz. "the aesthetic", the sophisticated hedonism of "Don Juan the Seducer" in *Either/Or*. The professor eschewed specific reading assignments as alien to our "existential freedom", so I exercised my existential freedom by leaving.

Another fascinating and charming professor, Robert Brumbaugh, was equally eccentric. He taught a whole course on one Platonic dialog, by far the most puzzling and difficult, the "Parmenides". His diversions were more memorable than his lectures. He was at home in ancient Greece and regaled us with tales of finding faded medieval copies of Plato's writings in the moldy basements of old monasteries and testing the hypothesis that they were mistakenly translated because the sound of the Greek letter epsilon, a short e ("eh"), was misinterpreted as the sound of the Greek letter eta, a long e ("ay"), which made the difference between the particles "deh" and "day" for probability and certainty, because the standard audible reference for that vowel that translators used for centuries was the bleat of a goat, but Turkish (Byzantine) goats bleat differently from Greek goats. He had spent a whole semester audibly dictating Greek texts in a round-ceilinged Byzantine scriptorium to see which words may have been misunderstood because of the acoustics.

Still another professor, Rulon Wells, was a walking encyclopedia of Aristotle. He had apparently organized every term, premise, conclusion, and inference in all of Aristotle's works and could find, connect, and use any of them instantly in his large portable reference system consisting of thousands of complexly classified four-by-six-inch note cards, a kind of paper computer bank.

Frederick Fitch taught symbolic logic, and he was like a computer himself, but his logic was much simpler, clearer, and more common-sensical to me than the other systems of symbolic or mathematical logic that had become popular, especially the standard one (Russell and Whitehead's *Principia Mathematica*). I had always hated math, and nearly flunked advanced algebra in high school, but I aced Fitch's exam.

The most eccentric and incompetent professor I ever had, whose name I could neither remember nor pronounce, and who, strangely, looked like he was made of straw, taught Buddhist philosophy at Yale. I wondered why I was the only student who signed up for his course. And I soon found out. He may have attained *inka* (certification of having attained Enlightenment by a *roshi* who had), but he was totally disorganized and almost unintelligible. I don't remember how I got a good grade. However, taking his course helped qualify me for a Danforth fellowship to Japan to study Zen Buddhism some years later.

When I began teaching at Villanova (my first teaching job) in 1961, I had transferred from Yale to Fordham (mainly to get more of Aquinas) and was still working on my PhD, and I took a course at the University of Pennsylvania from the only Thomist on the faculty there, a very old man who simply went through the first few articles of the *Summa* with me with slow and painful care, almost word for word. I was the only student in his class (again!).

❧ ❧ ❧

I know of no occupation that houses more diverse and inclusive people than university education. But their calls for "diversity, equity, and inclusion" almost always, in my experience, are really attacks on diversity, equity, and inclusion, both ideological and personal, a confusion of equity with equality, and an insistence on ideological uniformity and conformity to modernist liberal left-wing "progressive" semi-Marxist "woke" orthodoxy. The Italian Marxist philosopher Gramsci was a prophet when he said that Communism will not conquer the world at the ballot box or on the battlefield, but in the classroom.

Yes, I am a critic of the "diversity, equity, and inclusion" police, because I believe in all three of these things and they do not, any more than Robespierre and the "reign of terror" in the French Revolution believed in "liberty, equality, and fraternity" as they claimed they did. For them, DEI quickly became DIE. Both then and now, they are profoundly hypocritical. A "hypocrite" is not simply one who does not practice what he preaches (that's just a "sinner") but one who does not *believe* what he preaches. Like the "feminists" who hate and fear and resent all things feminine—Simone de Beauvoir, for example. Calling them "feminists" is like calling the largest tyranny in the world "the people's republic".

I am a happy, old, white, Gentile, American, heterosexual, conservative, religious, Christian, Catholic, Evangelical, traditional, dogmabelieving, hierarchical, authoritative, absolutistic, moralistic, repentant sinner. But I do not hate or fear or resent the unhappy, the young, Blacks, Asians, Hispanics, Jews, immigrants, gays, liberals, secularists, atheists, Protestants, modernists, progressives, skeptics, egalitarians, anti-authoritarians, relativists, immoralists, or unrepentant autoerotic narcissists. In fact, I love them, because my God loves them. But many of them hate me for being different from all those things that they are. I'm an antidisestablishmentarian. I am grateful, not hateful, to the "establishment" that is the rich and diverse culture that has given me Moses, Solomon, Homer, Sophocles, Socrates, Virgil, Jesus, Marcus Aurelius, Augustine, Aquinas, Dante, Shakespeare, Da Vinci, Bach, Beethoven, Chopin, Dickens, Dostoevsky, Tolstoy, Kierkegaard, Tolkien, and Mother Teresa, as well as Buddha, Confucius, and Lao Tzu. I shall defend them against the "culture warriors" who want to throw them down the Memory Hole of *1984*'s "Newspeak".

Some day, I may tell you what I *really* think about the "brave new world" of deconstructionism.

ૐ ૐ ૐ

Yale required my passing two foreign language tests. I aced the German one, but I was worried about the French, which I had tried to "get up" on my own by my rather feeble efforts. At Calvin the French course was "conversational" rather than bookish, and as I have mentioned I had to drop out because I was flunking. (I know now that my ADD gave me auditory processing problems.) By a gift of divine grace, the French exam at Yale was to translate into English a passage from the French translation of a little-known book by Heidegger (*Was ist dass—die Philosophie?*), in German, which I had recently read in English and remembered. (I found Heidegger's prose quite poetic; that's the only reason why I remembered it well.) So I passed a French test in English only by recognizing Heidegger's German.

Many years later, I experienced another triple play in language when my wife and I visited her father's native town in Italy (Cossignano). We knew little or no Italian, but we managed to converse with the non-English-speaking natives only because one of them knew French (as did my wife), and one of them knew German (as did I). It was a hilariously clumsy version of the Tower of Babel.

At Calvin I had discovered and fallen in love with Aquinas, and George Lindbeck was Yale's reigning expert on Aquinas. So I took his course. All spoke well of him, and he was, as expected, learned and reasonable as a philosopher, clear as a teacher, and charming as a human being; but his course just did not "click" with me. Perhaps the fact that he was a Lutheran instead of a Catholic had something to do with it, not directly but subconsciously. Perhaps I lusted for metaphysics but smelled Luther's nominalism; I don't know.

I transferred to Fordham after one year at Yale primarily to get more of Aquinas; and even though that was a stupid move from a pragmatic and "business" standpoint, since a Yale PhD would have given me many more prestigious choices and opportunities than a Fordham PhD, yet it was providentially right because I discovered there Father Norris Clarke, who like Saint Thomas himself had the wonder of a child and the logical mind of a medieval Scholastic. He was not just a great Thomist but a little Thomas. He was supernaturally patient with my simplistic abstractions and very gently helped me solve the puzzle of my Master's thesis: How can the act of existence itself be intelligible if essence is the principle of intelligibility and existence is really distinct from essence? (Yes, we philosophers really do care about such things. If we don't, who will?)

While at Yale, I met, befriended, roomed with, and transferred to Fordham the same year as, a very funny, eccentric, and wonder-full student named Marshall Dodge, who became famous for his *hilariously* funny recorded anthologies of Down East Maine humor entitled "Bert and I". Only a few years later he was tragically killed in Hawaii while riding a bike.

When I got my doctorate from Fordham, a few years later, at the graduation ceremony, when I returned to my seat robed in the glory of my PhD, I received a nugget of profound wisdom from my father-in-law, who was born in Italy and spoke broken English: "Peter, I'm not a Doctor of Philosophy like you, but I'd like to tell you my philosophy,

OK?" "Sure, Pop, what is it?" "Just always remember this: whatever you do and whichever way you turn, you always have an asshole behind you." It was what God said to Job a bit more elegantly.

My favorite sermon of all time has always been the two points in four words that God preached to Saint Catherine: "I'm God, you're not." We keep forgetting that second point.

22

God and Man at Yale

I arrived at Yale on Labor Day weekend of 1959 to memorably wintery, almost-freezing, temperatures. My very first day I rang the bell of the Dominican rectory early in the morning. A fat, short, jolly, Irish priest came downstairs in his bathrobe (I probably woke him up) and said, in a friendly way, "What can I do for you?" I replied, all bright-eyed and bushy-tailed, "Father, I want to become a Catholic." His reply, with a gently cynical smile, was: "Oh, that's nice. So who's the girl?" He was from Brooklyn.

Father Quinlan was delightful to be with. He had graduated 101st in his class of 101 seminarians and was pure practicality. I would come to him with questions from Saint Thomas Aquinas or Saint John of the Cross, and his answer was always: "Well, let's start with the old penny catechism, OK? We have to crawl before we can walk, and we have to walk before we can run." He didn't have all the answers, by a long shot, but he knew where to get them. His happy humor and his attitude taught me something about Catholicism that I needed more than ideas and answers: don't be more serious than God. If you doubt that God has a sense of humor, go not to the books but to the zoo. He put many gargoyles into his cathedral of a world for us: gooney birds and giraffes, ostriches and ocelots—and others. His whole world is other than any that we could ever imagine.

Yale at that time was rife with old Yankee anti-Catholic prejudices, and that made the Catholic community there strong, as the pagan Romans did to the early Christians. Even today, the Church is strongest where she is poor and persecuted (China, the Islamic world, Africa) and weakest where she is rich, established, and comfortable (Germany, Holland, Canada, the U.K., Ireland).

The chapel of Saint Thomas More at Yale was one of the few pieces of minimalist modern architecture that I loved, full of cool silver light. I joined its choir (which sang lots of Palestrina: pure gold) and its Gregorian chant group. This was another falling in love, and I still have, cherish, and sometimes even sing from my twenty-five-hundred-page Gregorian *Liber Usualis*.

I was impressed by the Dominicans, and still am, and I personally find their teaching "charism" and their creation-affirming spirituality more appealing than any other religious order's. I admired the history and educational achievements of the Jesuits, but when I tried Saint Ignatius of Loyola's *Spiritual Exercises* on my own, I found myself asking abstract philosophical questions about them rather than doing the practice or trying to imagine the details in the Gospel stories. It felt like "small talk", which I could never learn to do. I admired the Benedictines, too, especially after spending a week at a C. S. Lewis seminar in the Mojave Desert in Valyermo, California. (Other than that, I have never been on a retreat in my life, nor have I ever had a spiritual director. Not bragging, just complaining.)

I thought seriously of becoming a Dominican, but Father Quinlan told me of their wise regulation that new converts had to wait at least three years before they could be accepted as candidates. I never seriously considered becoming a parish priest—I knew my ordinary "bedside manner" was not winsome, for even at a young age I liked curmudgeons and disliked glad-handers—but I was drawn to the contemplative orders, so long as their fasts and penances were not too severe for my laziness. The Church was relaxing her rules for fasting, and I think that was a significant pastoral mistake. I was never big on fasting, and therefore needed it. I always thought of gluttony as the least serious of the Seven Deadly Sins, probably because I can eat anything I want and still stay skinny.

By the time I got to Yale, I was ready for Baptism because most of my theological questions had already been answered by all the Catholic apologetics that I had read. What deepened at Yale was my heart and my love of the Church and her beauties, more than my head and my acceptance of her teachings and her wisdom, which were already in place.

I chose February 2, which was then the feast of Saint Ignatius of Antioch, as my Baptism day. Most new Catholics romanticize martyrs like him. And then comes Monday morning.

Back then (1960), the Church "conditionally rebaptized" Protestants because she hoped, but did not presume and assume, that the

Protestant baptism was valid. I asked John, one of my Catholic class-mates at Yale, to be my godfather, and I asked the only Catholic woman I knew, Maria, to be my godmother.

I met Maria because she was dating my college friend Sam at the time, and I was "dating" the Church, strongly leaning toward a voca-tion. Sam had met Maria the previous summer in a way that was clearly providential for me. He had left his native Grand Rapids home for New York City and had spent a week fruitlessly looking for a summer job there. The day he was about to take the bus home, as he was entering the door of a restaurant for his last New York meal, the busboy was unceremoniously being forcibly exited, thrown out by the manager for stealing from the cash register. Sam instantly applied for his job and was accepted. So he lived in New York that sum-mer, made friends with the head waitress, met her daughter, started dating her, and phoned me (I was home in New Jersey for the sum-mer working as a gofer at my father's engineering firm) to set up a double date. I found my date, Marie, very nice, but there were no sparks; Sam's date, Maria, was pretty, smart, and funny, but—well, she was Sam's date, and I was "dating" the Church.

That fall, Sam returned to Calvin for his senior year, and I went to Yale. Sam wrote to me something like this: "I know you believe this Catholic stuff, and so does my girl Maria, and I know you are seriously contemplating becoming a priest, so I wonder if you could do me a favor and help me keep this relationship that I had in New York with Maria going. You're a better writer than I am, so could you write to Maria telling her what a good guy I am?"

I did just that, and I asked Maria, "What do you see in Sam that you don't see in any of the other guys at your school?" Maria wrote back, "Since I go to an all-girls' college, I think you can figure out the answer to that question. But why don't you come down to New York some weekend and meet my family and we can talk about Sam?" I did, and I increasingly fell in love with Maria and with a vocation to the other and even more important kind of fatherhood, while Sam started dating and eventually married the girl I had dated casually at Calvin.

I remember exactly where I was when I decided to marry Maria instead of the priesthood: on the southwest corner of Amsterdam Ave-nue and Eighty-Ninth Street facing east (*ad orientem*). Maria, meanwhile, learned from her mailman that she was in love with me when he asked her why she was always more eager to get my letters than Sam's.

At the time of my Baptism, I was still contemplating becoming a Dominican, as Maria knew; and she joked to the priest, Father Quinlan, "Father, what if I fall in love with this guy? Can he marry his godmother?" The answer was: "Nope. The Church forbids it. It's like spiritual incest. When those laws were made, being a godparent was a very serious thing. But the law is still on the books, so you'd have to get a special dispensation from Rome for that." A year later, we both asked Father Quinlan, "Can you get that dispensation for us?" And he did. So I married my godmother.

And she has done her godmotherly job of spiritual service to me ever since, seeing through all my rationalisms and faithfully loving me despite my psychological clumsiness. If you've ever seen the deservedly popular and beloved BBC comedy *Doc Martin*, she is Louisa, and I am the Doc.

Immediately after my Baptism, I received my First Communion. It was a great grace, partly because it was a blessed *absence* of great *emotional* graces. I felt absolutely nothing but a total silence. My thoughts and feelings are usually racing through my mind like roller skaters, but at that moment the whole world was still, as in the silent night in the little town of Bethlehem. I am grateful for the lack of feelings, and for God's wise reason for it: to make my faith-walk independent of my feeling-crutches. The object of faith is not feelings but truth, and the subject and agent of faith is will, not feelings. The will is like the ocean, and the feelings are like the waves. The ocean is always reliably there even though the waves are high one day and low the next. And there is more spiritual power in the dark troughs of the waves, in the lack of what Saint John of the Cross calls "sensible consolations", than in the crests, where the fun and the whitewater are.

My Confirmation came shortly after. My major memory from it is my disappointment that the Church had discontinued the centuries-old ceremonial slap on the face by the bishop that symbolized our entrance into spiritual warfare and conflict. I wanted to be readied for combat, to follow in the footsteps of Saint Ignatius of Antioch. (It's amazingly easy to romanticize struggle and suffering when you are outside it rather than inside. In other words, it's amazingly easy to be a fool.)

23

Politics

This is a strange chapter because it is about what I chose *not* to put in this book rather than about what I chose to put in it. But some readers will notice and wonder at the absence, and I want to explain its reason.

I have said a lot about philosophy and a lot about religion but nothing about politics (or economics, or sociology) throughout this book; and I shall continue to say nothing about these three associated subjects, because joining the Church is very different from joining a political party, or even becoming a citizen of another country. It's more like getting married or joining the army. Today the majority of scholars, sociologists, psychologists, anthropologists, and journalists see politics as more powerful, more practical, more realistic, more true, and more important than religion, while those who actually believe what their religion teaches (whether it's Christianity or another religion) must see things in the opposite way: that our politics is only our human invention and fashion, whether it is monarchical, aristocratic, or democratic, but religion transcends all mere human invention as the sky transcends the earth.

Therefore, when religion lets itself be influenced by politics, it always gets corrupted, while when politics lets itself be influenced by religion, it gets sanctified. This is true of all true religion. What is true religion? The heart of all true religion is a relationship with God, however well or poorly God is known. This is true of all three Western religions explicitly, but it is true of Eastern religions, too, even though they have a far less adequate concept of the God we are to surrender to. It is also true despite the fact that all three Western religions have a very compromised historical record in regard to practicing this total surrender to God rather than to politics.

That does not mean that politics is not important. It is an important dimension of our "mission field". And it certainly does not mean that the social or collective dimension of our lives, both private (especially the family and ancestry) and public (especially politics) is not important. I am by nature an introvert, an only child, and a "loner", but I cannot and do not deny that for a Catholic, salvation is essentially social as well as essentially individual. For we are not first saved as individuals and then put into the Ark. Salvation *is* being put into the Ark of Salvation. Thus the Church's principle that "outside the Church there is no salvation." For the Church is not only the visible institutional Church but also "the *Mystical* Body of Christ".

On the other hand, we are not baptized *en masse*. I saw what claimed to be a collective Jehovah's Witnesses baptism once, with a fire hose. No. We are no more baptized en masse or apostasize en masse than we are born en masse or die en masse.

We choose as individuals, but we are chosen to be God's family, as we are born into our human family. For our religion, unlike our political party, is God's invention, not ours. That is the only reason why she is infallible. Protestants, of course, do not believe that, and also, significantly, do not call her "she". (But at least some of them still do believe that the Bible is infallible.) The Church, the Ark of Salvation, unlike the ark of Noah, which imperfectly symbolizes it, is not a work of human technology. She is the Body of Christ. We are "in-corporated" (literally, in-bodied) into this Body as her "members", so that we become organs in an organism, not individuals in an organization. Christ is not our CEO.

But political parties are only human inventions. Most Christians today are inside out and upside down; they are religious about their politics and political about their religion. Paradoxically, the secular world's prioritizing politics and ideology has infected Christians more today, when we celebrate the "separation of Church and State", than in the Middle Ages, when the Church "controlled" the State.

There is a very simple argument for the priority of the individual over the state and politics. It is the simple fact that every individual who ever lived will live forever. We are immortal; states, nations, parties, cultures, civilizations, even the stars, are mortal. Democrats and Republicans don't go to Heaven; Christians do. "The image of God" is in persons, not societies. (But it *is* in marriage: see Gen 1:27

and Mt 19:3–6.) Every person, from Adam to the last man on earth, will experience either the Beatific Vision of God or the Miserific Vision of Satan, either light or heat, light or fire, light or darkness, eternally. This fact almost trivializes politics. It also trivializes philosophy, which is much more important than politics.

24

My Parents' Reaction to My Conversion

My psychological immaturity and stupidity were so massive that I somehow thought that when I told my parents of my discovery that the true Church was Catholic, they would be open to hearing about it. I was shocked when my father was shocked—so shocked that the first thing he said in reply was that I had just broken his heart. I think it would have been less hurtful to him if I had become a Buddhist or an atheist.

I had made the inexcusable mistake of shielding them for years from my gradual growing interest in things Catholic. For a long time I subconsciously thought, "This phase will probably pass; why disturb their peace?" And when I told Father Quinlan of their reaction, he wisely advised me to give them time to deal with me by not telling them I was already conditionally baptized as a Catholic but to allow them into the dialogue as if I were still on the way. So I did, and months of very difficult arguments ensued. The fact that I had surprised and hurt them so deeply surprised and hurt me very deeply. My theology was mature, but my psychology was very immature. For I failed to empathize with the betrayal my parents must have felt when their one and only son, whom they sent to Calvin, the safest place in the world for training in Calvinism, became the very last thing they ever wanted him to become: a Catholic. They did not and could not understand how this could possibly have made me more, not less, Christocentric, closer to rather than farther from the Lord who was their Lord as well as mine. When a Jew becomes a Christian and insists that he is now more Jewish rather than less, he cannot expect any of his fellow Jews even to comprehend that, much less accept it. I was a fool to hope that my parents would understand. I forgot that when a Muslim tells his family that he now loves Allah more because he has become a Christian, the reaction is that he will be disowned, exiled, or executed.

My "deal" with my parents was that I would be open to their persuasion and share my journey with them in the present rather than simply presenting it to them as a past *fait accompli*. I attended their church with them, which was not a problem or a hypocrisy because I believed everything they believed and more. I had many long conversations with Dad, most of them exasperating and a few of them enlightening, including one with the great Calvinist theologian at Westminster Seminary in Philadelphia, Cornelius Van Til, who was very gracious and intelligent, but not persuasive. We disagreed philosophically as well as theologically. Like Karl Barth, he was suspicious of my heroes: Socrates, Plato, Aristotle, Aquinas, natural reason, universal rational natural moral law, metaphysics, real universals, essences, natures, natural theology, and the analogy of being—in other words, *Logos*.

My mother's reaction was as sorrowful as my father's but less argumentative. Once, when my father and I were arguing about Purgatory, she listened in and then said to him, "John, I think Peter really believes the same thing we do." My father was surprised, "Of course he doesn't. We don't believe in Purgatory." "No," she said, "we don't. But we believe in everything in the Bible, and I think Peter is saying that the reasons he believes in Purgatory are in the Bible, too: first, that we are all sinners ('If we say we have no sin, we deceive ourselves, and the truth is not in us'—1 Jn 1:8); and second, that nothing sinful can enter Heaven, only what is holy ('Nothing unclean shall enter it'—Rev 21:27); and third, that there's no compromise between sin and holiness, but a great gap between them, right?" She looked at me questioningly, and I said, "Right." "Well, then, God will have to do *something* to us when we die to make us totally holy, so if we don't want to call that Purgatory and Peter does, aren't we just arguing over a word?" My father never brought up the subject again.

I was very impressed by their acceptance of Maria and our marriage and by their genuine love of Maria despite the radical contrast not only in religion but also in culture. Maria's family was a large, loud, Italian and Russian family that drank, gambled, laughed, and swore. Mine was a small, quiet, almost "American Gothic" sort of pious and polite Puritan family. I was the only child on my father's side of the family, and my mother's side was not very close to us. When I told my father that Maria and I wanted six kids, he was very happy. "The doctor told your mother after you were born that she really shouldn't have any more kids, and I'm very glad for you that you want more children than we had." When I heard the word "more", I thought that that word covered all the differences between his Protestantism and my Catholicism: more dogmas and creeds and sacraments and liturgies and saints and angels and authority. And more kids, and thus more pleasures and more pains. But pains are interruptions of pleasures; pleasures are not interruptions of pains.

A few years after our marriage Mom came down with Parkinson's disease and became increasingly passive and incapacitated. But even when she could no longer talk, she could sing her favorite hymns. My faithful and saintly father gave her total home care, with only a little relief, for twenty years.

When my father was eighty-nine, he hurt his back shoveling snow, had a very painful operation, a very slow recovery in rehab, caught pneumonia in the nursing home, and died. I was present for his death, as I hadn't been for Mom's. It left an enormous hole in the universe. But he was ready. His last words, not with mouth but with his body, were a smile and a handclasp when I said, "Go under the Mercy, Dad."

My father, I am convinced, played an after-death role in getting us our cottage on Martha's Vineyard, "the Purple Angel". The Vineyard town of Oak Bluffs, like Ocean Grove in New Jersey, had been a Methodist campground and retreat center in the nineteenth century and was similarly famous for its hundreds of little "gingerbread houses" with fanciful and colorful trim. Our little cottage is only nine hundred square feet but sleeps eight! The times our family spent in Ocean Grove were the happiest in my childhood, and I am convinced Dad's prayers arranged for us to continue to enjoy that happiness in the Ocean Grove of Massachusetts. Here are three reasons for that belief: not only did we buy the cottage with the money we inherited from the sale of Dad's house, and not only did we get our cottage through a very providential set of unusual circumstances, a very tiny open window of opportunity, but we also just happened to sign the lease on the exact anniversary of his death. (We realized that only afterward.) Because of "the Communion of Saints", when they die and go to Heaven, parents don't forget their children but continue to pray for them and watch over them. Heaven is much closer to earth, and earth closer to Heaven, than we think.

My father made two remarkable religious admissions to me before he died. When his church, the Reformed Church in America, like other Protestant denominations, changed its teachings on a number of issues and compromised with "modernism", he said to me, "When the New Testament Church in Jerusalem decided an issue, they wrote, 'It has seemed good to the Holy Ghost and to us' (Acts 15:28, KJV). That's the language of *authority*. I have to admit that sometimes your church looks more like the New Testament church than mine does. Yours still uses that language and mine doesn't."

The other admission, years later, was: "Peter, I still disagree with your theology, but I believe you are trying to follow our Lord's leading, and I understand that that's why you became a Catholic, and I have to respect your motives for your choice even though I deeply disagree with your choice. I believe God is somehow using you in ways I can't see." That may sound quite reasonable and easy to say for most people, but if you knew how rock-solid a Calvinist my father was, you would be as deeply impressed as I was at that admission. How remarkable that we both had such deep respect for each other at the same time as deeply disagreeing about the issues. We both believed "Hate the heresy but love the heretic" as well as "Hate the sin but love the sinner." The principle was "hate the disease but love the patient." In fact, "Hate the disease (whether the disease was cancer, heresy, or sin) *because* you love the patient (the cancerous body, the heretic, or the sinner)." The two easier and more popular alternatives are to love both or to hate both. The typical dangers of the Left and of the Right.

My father was adventurous, my mother was not. My mother was a happy homebody, humble and simple. I suspect in God's eyes she was closer to the center of all things than the rest of us. In those days, this was the usual pattern that distinguished most men and most women. If that pattern was too rigid and oppressive—which it probably was, in itself—it did not usually feel that way; and if our present opening up of far more opportunities to women is a liberating and happy thing—which it probably is, in itself—it does not usually feel that way, especially for the "liberated" women. No one would have believed me if I went back in a time machine to the forties or fifties and told them that one-third of the babies conceived in America were aborted.

25

Fordham

I transferred from Yale to Fordham partly to be near Maria but primarily to study Saint Thomas Aquinas. And I was not disappointed, mainly because of Father Norris Clarke, S.J. His understanding of Thomas was deep, large, open, clear, and broad. The most difficult part of Aquinas, I thought, was not his theology but his philosophy, and, within his philosophy, his metaphysics. Father Clarke made that metaphysics alive. I discovered later that his informal handouts for his metaphysics class had been circulating among graduate students and also among many Thomist teachers as a far better textbook alternative than any book in print. When Father Clarke discovered this, he was persuaded to collect them into a finished manuscript and publish it, as *The One and the Many*, which is the only textbook I have ever seen that also qualifies as a masterfully creative philosophical system.

Aquinas has a unique gift of being two opposite things, clear and profound, at the same time. What other philosopher can even closely match that? Father Clarke had the same gift. He loved to "think on his feet" and be open to, and in genuine dialog about, ideas that we thought were dead and dull. And not only in Thomas but also in modern philosophers, for instance, his discovery of Gabriel Marcel, who was not a Thomist but a Personalist and a phenomenologist. Clarke's work is a creative and original synthesis of Thomistic metaphysics with modern Personalism, a synthesis of the best of the old and the best of the new, the objective and the subjective, the substantive and the relational, the cosmic and the personal, the ontological and the existential, which was summarized especially in his little masterpiece *Person and Being*. Like Pope Saint John Paul II's "Theology of the Body", it's not easy but it "hooks" you, fascinates you, and convinces you.

Father Clarke patiently guided my convoluted MA thesis on "the intelligibility of the act of existence"; and at my PhD dissertation defense, when I received a withering attack by a brilliant but wild relativist who was exemplifying Nietzsche's "will to power" and thought my position far too "conservative" to pass, he saved me by calmly refuting all the wild objections and offering mediation when he saw that I was surprised at the attack and would have attacked back, further alienating my enemy, who had to sign off on my degree.

I was also fortunate to take courses from Balduin Schwarz (the favorite student of the great Dietrich von Hildebrand, who had retired the same year I entered Fordham). These courses on the history of philosophy gave me the depth and breadth, the profundity and span, that specialized courses leave behind, plus a lifelong friendship and respect for his son Stephen, a fine philosopher himself, a careful and clear phenomenologist, the author of the best and clearest introduction I know to philosophical questions by a combination of the techniques of phenomenology and analytic philosophy, and another book that is the most convincing and complete refutation of abortion I know. When he was a child, he and his parents escaped from their native Austria, when Balduin and von Hildebrand were on Hitler's "hit list". The family was chased across Europe by the Nazis, hidden by French monks, and eventually escaped to America.

At Fordham I came to love the Eastern Catholic liturgy of Saint John Chrystostom, which was celebrated by the Russian Center Jesuits there. The division between East and West, Orthodoxy and Catholicism, was never an either/or issue for me. They were two wings of the same bird, while Protestantism was a man-made airplane. Or, to use another analogy, they were the two lungs of the same Body, while Protestantism was a respirator.

26

Villanova

When we married, Maria and I drew two circles around where our parents lived (Paterson, New Jersey, and the Bronx, only twenty miles from each other). One was fifty miles away from home, which was too close, and the other was three hundred miles away, which was too far. We agreed to live somewhere between those two circles so that we could be close enough to our parents to visit easily and often but not so close that we would be expected too easily and too often. The two cities in that area were Philadelphia and Boston. So the first job I accepted was at Villanova, in Philadelphia, where I taught from 1961 to 1965, and the second was at Boston College, where I've been since 1965.

While teaching at Villanova, I also did a lot of moonlighting, at Haverford, La Salle, and Saint Peter's in Jersey City, and later, in Boston, at three different seminaries, as well as many adult education courses. When I started teaching, $4,500 was my annual salary and nine courses per year (four each semester and one in summer school) was the standard load. One year, with all the moonlighting, I actually taught nineteen different courses at seven different schools. I also drove a taxi one summer to make ends meet. Today, a full-time load for full professors is three courses a year, and full professors make over six figures.

When I first taught at Villanova, I taught four sections of Logic, from the textbook chosen, not by the professor or by the department chairman, but by the bookstore manager. One of my classes contained some of the football team, who would routinely fall asleep during class. They had spent nearly every waking hour on the field being drilled so hard that garbage cans were provided for the throwups. They were no more interested in defining a football than I was in carrying one.

The students at Haverford, where I moonlighted, were very con-
scientious, and the lowest grade I ever gave there was a B. It is a
Quaker school, and one of their pacifist students once stumped me
in a short informal debate: "Is Jesus your absolute authority?" "Yes."
"If you believed that it was impossible that Jesus would ever do x,
would you ever do x?" "No." "Do you believe it is possible that Jesus
might fire a machine gun to deliberately kill an enemy soldier?" "No.
I see your point. Pacifism 'feels' right. But if you were the President
of the United States and the Russian premier (who at the time was
the bellicose Nikita Khrushchev, who banged his shoe on the desk
at the UN and threatened, 'We will bury you!') discovered that you
were a Quaker pacifist, and sent his fleet across the Atlantic, would
you send out our navy to stop him by force?" "No." "And when he
sailed up the Potomac and marched into the oval office and demanded
you resign, what would you say to him?" "I would say, 'Welcome,
my brother in Christ.' And my only weapon would be the love of
Christ and His Gospel." I was impressed by his consistency. But
he did not convince me of pacifism. What he did convince me of
was that for a Christian there had to be a double standard: pacifism
and even martyrdom could be admirable for individuals, but not for
nations, which have a moral obligation to protect their citizens from
bullies, as good fathers do for their children.

I do not remember any new and significant religious discoveries or
insights during the years immediately after my conversion, only two
great literary discoveries: *The Lord of the Rings* and *The Brothers Kara-
mazov*, the two greatest novels ever written. The skeletal structure
of the Faith was clear and complete; now I had to add the muscles,
nerves, and skin. I became more interested in how to live the Faith,
how to become a saint, than how to think it. Needless to say, I did a
much better job thinking it than living it.

While I was at Villanova, Vatican II turned the altar and the language around. I neither rejoiced nor complained: like the Church
herself, I like both old things and new things. Both Gregorian chant
and Gothic cathedrals were once new things. And all the things
affirmed by the decrees of this newest of Church councils—a "pastoral" counsel—were old things, traditional doctrines and practices,
just newly pastor-ized. Since I do not tell time with a syllogism, I do
not tell truth with a clock. Some old things are bad, and some are

good. Slavery is bad, and anaesthetics are good. Some new things are bad, and some are good. Nazism was bad, and the Universal Declaration of Human Rights was good. Ambrose Bierce, in *The Devil's Dictionary*, defines a "conservative" as "one who is enamoured of old evils" and a "progessive" as "one who wants to replace them with new ones."

It was neither the best of times nor the worst of times. In 1961, you could get a good little steak dinner for 99 cents. Our three-room suburban apartment was $85 a month. Most middle-class families owned their own home and had more than two kids. The father was paid what the Church called a "family wage", and most mothers did not have to work outside the house. Kids still saw summer as vacation time. There were no mass shootings or terrorists. But there was a rather big "but": the world was worried about a nuclear war, and Communism ruled almost half the world. We sons of Adam and daughters of Eve always seem to manage to come up with something big to worry about. I wonder whether the real but subconscious reason we always keep inventing new worries is to keep our minds distracted from what is a much bigger and permanent one, which we fear to admit we are really worried about: death, the Last Judgment, and eternity. For what, after all, can be bigger than that?

My friends at Villanova included Clement, a student from Tanzania/Tanganyika who could not be persuaded to believe in the law of non-contradiction or to disbelieve that "devil's food cake" was literally from or for devils. Here is a typical argument that I heard between him and Bob, a very smart logic professor:

"Clement, did you see Professor X on campus today?"

"Yes."

"Did he say anything about his final exam that you flunked?"

"No, I did not."

"You mean *he* did not."

"No, I mean I did not. I did not see him."

"But a minute ago you said you did see him."

"Yes."

"Well, you must have lied. Which is the truth?"

"Whatever you please. But I do not lie. I am not a liar."

"But Clement, one of those two things you said must be a lie: that you did or that you didn't see Professor X."

"No, there is no such thing as a lie."

"Clement, look at my hand. How many fingers do you see on it?"

"Five."

"Good. Now listen to me: I'm telling you I have six fingers on that hand. Am I not lying?"

"No. It is your hand, not mine."

"I say it is not my hand. It is yours. Am I not telling a lie?"

"No."

"Why not?"

"Because there is no such thing as a lie."

"But if there is no such thing as a lie, then it must be a lie that there is such a thing as a lie."

"No. There is no such thing as a lie. Not even a lie about whether there is a lie."

"Well, I say there is."

"I hear you. I understand you. You believe there is, and I believe there is not."

"Am I wrong, then, to believe there is not?"

"No. No one is wrong."

"But if no one is wrong, as you say, then it is wrong for me to think that some one is wrong."

"No. That is not wrong."

"Why not?"

"Because no one is wrong. See? I am as consistent as you are. I stand here, and you stand there, and we both stand."

"If that is all we can do, then what good is logical argument?"

"It is good for nothing, unless you want to turn your brain into a pretzel."

I think Clement flunked every true/false or multiple choice test that he ever took. I don't think it possible that he was as confused as it seems, or that he was some kind of a pantheistic mystic. I think he was just playing a game with us. His typical answer to an either/or question was "Whatever you please." Perhaps that was the response he learned to make to his colonial overlords as a child.

27

Boston College

I always wanted to live in Boston. Boston is a pretty city. It is historic, walkable, and "classy"—like Philadelphia, or a small New York. Boston had Fenway Park, the Celtics, the Boston Symphony Orchestra, beautiful islands and beaches, and more colleges and universities per person and per square mile than any other major city in America.

So as soon as Boston called with a job opening, I answered, and I've never regretted it. I've been happy here for almost sixty years now (since 1965). The Jesuits are almost always intelligent, sophisticated, caring, and personable. And as everyone knows, they also contain more "dissenters" (we used to call them "heretics") than any other religious order. Students gibe that "BC" means "Barely Catholic". One incoming student actually once asked me, in innocent ignorance, "Is BC Catholic or Jesuit?" Nearly everyone in our Philosophy Department (the largest in the country) is a practicing Catholic, and there are many great Jesuits here who also eat all the food Mother Church puts on our plate, so I have had the privilege of feeling "at home" here as a Catholic—and also of feeling that I am on a foreign mission field among pagans, since student life typically centers on parties, sex, and alcohol. BC has fifteen thousand students in all its schools, the majority of whom "identify" as Catholics, but only a minority go to Mass. My simplest definition of "Catholic identity" is that "you are what you eat." To be in His Body is to have His Body in you.

You can get an excellent education at BC, both religiously and academically, if you really want to and if you make the effort to be discriminating among professors, courses, and friends. That d-word used to be a compliment, with no racist connotations. Our department (philosophy) is so "discriminating" that we admit only five out of between 120 and 200 applicants to our PhD program each year. Not only my department in particular but also the university in general seem to me to have always manifested great friendliness and cooperation, excellent academic quality, and none of the in-house sniping and backbiting that you find in many other prestigious universities. All undergraduates still must take two semesters of philosophy and two of theology, and these courses remain very popular. One year we had four hundred philosophy majors, more than any other college or university in America. We still have over two hundred, even with the drastic decline of the humanities.

I've been able to teach pretty much whatever I want and have invented over fifty different new courses. I see the relation between my philosophy and my religious faith as something distinct from both evangelism, on the one hand, and secular neutrality, on the other hand. I see philosophizing as the honest love of truth (and goodness and beauty) wherever it is, the willingness to follow the argument wherever it leads, and the love of the greatest of questions, especially the "existential" questions of life and death, good and evil, wisdom and folly, God and man, certainty and uncertainty. I look on Socrates, Plato, Aristotle, Plotinus, Augustine, Boethius, Anselm, Aquinas, Pascal, Kierkegaard, Newman, James, Heidegger, Marcel, Buber, Wittgenstein, Von Hildebrand, and Chesterton as my friends (not to mention Homer, Sophocles, Dante, Shakespeare, Dickens, Austen, Wordsworth, Dostoevsky, Tolstoy, Eliot, Lewis, and Tolkien), and I look at the Sophists, Ockham, Machiavelli, Descartes, Hobbes, Spinoza, Hume, Kant, Hegel, Russell, Dewey, Mill, Marx, Freud, Nietzsche, and Sartre as worthy opponents. Not many people are privileged to have that many close friends among the great ones.

When I first came to Boston College, I was put on a committee that was to design a whole new curriculum. We met weekly for two years, and at the end issued a massive, detailed report with many concrete recommendations. It was totally ignored; it had been a mere "paper trail" to look good to the Board of Trustees and to government agencies that were ready to give us the right money if we had the right look. I have distrusted and avoided committees ever since. I made a great deal with my friendly department chairman to teach an extra course every year for free if I could be kept off all time-consuming committees. A deal made in Heaven. The three most important things you need to know about committees are these: (1) Arabs define a camel as a horse designed by a committee. (2) Someone (Churchill?) famously said that nothing great in the entire history of the world was ever done by a committee. (3) There was a New York Broadway comedy many decades ago entitled *The Creation of the Universe* in which an up-to-date God designed the whole universe by committees. It resembled *Waiting for Godot*, *Catch-22*, and *One Flew Over the Cuckoo's Nest* combined.

۶۵ ۶۵ ۶۵

In the next chapter, instead of relating the next sixty years of my personal or family life, I will answer a harder but more pointed, philosophical, and profound question. (I love hard questions and hate easy ones, especially from interviewers.) The question is: What have I learned about the Catholic faith in the last sixty years that I did not know or appreciate as a new convert?

New converts (and "reverts", too) are always more appreciative and enthusiastic than "cradle Catholics" because we appreciate everything best by contrast. (This is also part of the answer to "the problem of evil"—God lets us suffer for the sake of the greater joy of deliverance.) We appreciate food best after hunger, wealth after poverty, light after darkness, and life itself after a brush with death. We also appreciate faith more after doubt, and wisdom after foolishness.

28

Perspective

What Have I Learned in the Last Sixty Years?

I do not know how much, or to what extent, I would have learned these lessons if I had remained a Calvinist for the last sixty years, for they are all primarily personal issues, issues of religion rather than theology, issues about my personal relationship with my Lord. The change was not like the change from barrenness to pregnancy but like the change from an appetizer to the main course. Calvinism is a form of Protestantism, and Protestantism is a form of Christianity, and Christianity is essentially believing and trying to live the first, the earliest, of all Christian creeds, "Jesus Christ is Lord" (Phil 2:11).

So how has my mind changed after I started eating the main course?

1. I have learned that the Lordship of Christ, though necessarily a lordship over the mind, is most importantly a lordship over the will and living and loving. Thus, practical questions about the will and love are not merely spinoffs, corollaries, consequences, and deductions from theoretical questions about the mind and truth (though they are that, too) but are themselves the most important questions of all. One step closer to fulfilling God's will and becoming a saint is more important than a thousand steps closer to becoming the greatest theologian or philosopher in the world.

2. I have learned that I am a spoiled brat, a coddled kid, a self-indulgent, weak-willed, outraged, and whiney complainer when I bump into the obstacles, frustrations, and sufferings that God in His mercy and wisdom sends my way in relatively small amounts. I say this not only when I compare myself as I am with what God insists I become ("be ye perfect"—Mt 5:48, KJV), but also when I compare myself with many other people who often suffer far more and

complain far less, who pray more passionately and live more charita-
bly than I—and not all of them are Christians. I have had an easy life,
with far more joys than sufferings. I have the very life of Christ (*zoe*)
in me through faith and the sacraments, yet I still seem to live and
react 99 percent of the time from "the flesh" (*bios*) and only 1 percent from "the Spirit" (*zoe*), as is evident from my first, spontaneous
reaction to all temptations, whether temptations to pride, despair,
anger, defeatism, resentment, frustration, laziness, lust, impatience,
or self-indulgence. I have a long, long way to go, and my tiny appe-
tizers of Purgatory here on earth are going to have to be magnified
many times in my post-mortem completion of Purgatory. I anticipate
its joys (the infallible certainty of salvation and a sinless and non-
rebellious will) as well as its pains. I look forward to being able to say,
like Saint Lawrence, tortured on a barbecue spit, "Let my body be
turned; one side is broiled enough."

3. If the essence of Protestantism, or Evangelicalism, is a personal
relationship with Christ as Lord and Savior, I appreciate Protestantism more now than I did as a Protestant. Catholics agree with Protestants that Christ is "what it's all about"; they just disagree about what
is contained in that "all". Because I now see that one thing from the
standpoint of the whole thing (i.e., the whole Catholic thing), I now
see that that one thing is the point of the whole thing. It is the foundation, the center, and the end of the whole building.

4. I have learned to expect less of people. I cannot expect anyone
else to duplicate the love of my parents. I have learned to salute the
uniform, not the person wearing it, even when it comes to priests,
bishops, and even popes. There are great saints among all three of
those groups, but also sinners. Only eleven of the first twelve bishops
were saints. (Judas was the other.)

5. I have also learned to see the Church, not primarily as a large ship
of fallible fools (which she is) or a flock of stubborn sheep (which she is)
or as the jackass He chose to ride to show us who we are (which is also
true), but a great, glorious thing, a beautiful thing, a divine miracle, an
extension of the Incarnation, a Catholic and catholic (universal) thing,
spread out in time and space and containing all time and space rather
than being contained by them. It is in fact the reason for the Creation
of the universe, which is only our larger placenta. Like Christ and like
each of us, the Church is both visible and invisible, both human and

divine, both a painful and ugly thing and the beautiful and immaculate Bride of Christ.

When, at Calvin, I decided to become a Catholic, I had not knowingly ever talked face to face with someone I knew to be a believing Catholic, only to the dead ones I met through their books. It was an unusual path, but it was the right one for me as a natural Platonist: seeing the visible in light of the invisible rather than vice versa.

6. I have learned the importance of loving the sinner even while hating the sin, even (or rather, especially) regarding those whose sins are most flagrant and visible. They—we—are all both active sinners and sin's victims. Enlightenment can come instantly; the compassion usually takes time and experience.

7. I have learned to rely on the sacraments, especially Holy Communion and Confession, as indispensable, as the most important things in the world. The beauty of a world without wars is far less transformative than the ugliness of a world without sacraments.

8. I have learned the fragility of reason as well as the blindness of emotion.

9. I have learned the beauty and power of Mary, and that "the Church's Marian dimension is more primary than her Petrine dimension", as Pope Saint John Paul II the Great has said.

10. I have learned the wisdom of the Church's traditional and contemporary teachings about sexual morality, and especially the "Theology of the Body". I see my society committing suicide through all the sacraments of the sexual revolution, especially divorce, which destroys its own most fundamental foundation, marriage and the family; and I seem to see many in the Church working for that same end by quietly and cowardly conforming to the world rather than courageously correcting it.

11. I have learned that literature, my first love, is more powerful than philosophy; that stories are more powerful than theories or arguments. The Gospel is a story—"good *news*"—rather than a philosophy.

12. I have learned the necessity of suffering and sorrow in order to know God and to become holy. That was the hardest and perhaps the most necessary lesson of all.

13. I have learned that Christ is cosmic, that Christ is the key to everything, the center of everything.

14. I have learned that the essence of faith is personal trust rather than intellectual belief, which is only one of its dimensions. Trust is not essentially an emotion, any more than love is.

15. I have learned the syllogism that will save my sanity and my soul: the Romans 8:28 principle that since God is infinitely good, infinitely wise, and infinitely powerful, it necessarily follows that all things work together for good to those who are His children who love Him and are loved by Him. For His will is always perfect and ours is not.

16. I have learned that love is not just one thing but everything and that it is stronger than death, and harder. It is not soft and sweet. For it is what God is made of.

17. I have learned that writing books is very easy and, since it is a grace from God, joyful.

18. I have learned that angels are our best friends and our big brothers and our defense against the big bullies from Hell. Without them we are chopped liver. They are close. They fly and swim in our minds like birds in the air or fish in the sea.

19. I have learned that not my sufferings but my sins are my worst enemies.

20. I have learned that "Thy will be done" is sufficient for it means: "Give us what (a) You (b) infallibly (c) know we (d) need rather than what (a) we (b) fallibly (c) feel we (d) want."

21. I have learned that lists like these are always radical over-simplifications.

29

Retrospective

What Am I Most Grateful for in My Life?

This seems to be an appropriate question now that my life is nearly over and some view of the whole of it becomes more possible.

Saint Thomas, asked that question in his relatively old age, replied, with the unselfconscious humility of a saint, that he was grateful for the fact that he had understood everything he had ever read.

I certainly cannot say that. But a similar, though much simpler, grace was given to me from the earliest of my memories: to have no doubts at all that truth was objective and absolute; to refuse to give an inch to the two great modern heresies, the heresy of the priority of subjective feelings over objective truth and the heresy of the "social construction" of values (moral positivism and subjectivism), of truth ("my truth" versus "your truth"), of human nature itself (e.g., Marxism), of sex (the "trans" insanity now being pushed by all the media mouths), and even of being itself. These are sins not merely against good philosophy but against previously universal common sense and sanity, and they characterize only insane asylums and prestigious universities.

I was never even a little enamored of or tempted by Kant's "Copernican Revolution in philosophy", which makes *logos* (truth, meaning, form, structures, intelligibility, essences) the knowing subject's determination of the known object rather than vice versa. I loved the cartoon about the two castaways retrieving a message in a bottle from the ocean, who show at first happy, hopeful faces, but whose faces fall like Adam and Eve when they read it. They discover that "It's only from us."

178

I immediately detected and admired C. S. Lewis' objectivism, and I loved his satire on subjectivism in the chapter on the apostate bishop in *The Great Divorce* who denies objective truth, and his absolutely serious call for intellectual honesty in "Man or Rabbit", the most fundamental thing he ever wrote.

I am grateful for the grace by which I avoided popular ideologies. I was never in love with the demands of the passengers on this "ship of fools" for "equality" with their Divine Captain or His authorities or even with each other. I am happy not only to accept but to love hierarchy. I find it delightful to find myself in the company of both my superiors and my inferiors because that encourages the two greatest virtues, humility and charity.

$$\approx \quad \approx \quad \approx$$

I am also grateful that as I get older I get simpler. My favorite prayer has become the shortest and simplest one I ever heard, Saint Faustina's "Jesus, I trust in You." That is quite sufficient. For everything.

I wish my heart and will were as simple and holy as Aquinas', so that with my whole heart and soul I could reply as he did to the question Christ asked him, "You have written well of me, Thomas; what will you have as your reward?" His answer was: *"Non nisi te, domine"*, "Nothing but Yourself, Lord." My loves are nowhere nearly that tamed and unified and simplified. But my mind is, or at least passionately wants to be. I do not love God with my whole heart, but with my whole heart I want to love God with my whole heart.

God has a different task for each of us (that's why there are so many of us), and all these tasks are opportunities to practice obeying the fundamental commandment of "Thy will be done", the surrender that is the secret of joy.

$$\approx \quad \approx \quad \approx$$

I want to add a point that will sound surprising in light of my title *From Calvinist to Catholic* and in light of my criticisms of Calvinism in the book. I want to thank Calvin and Calvinists, sincerely and from my heart, for their strong affirmation of the absolute sovereignty of God and its most famous corollary, predestination, which is scriptural

(Rom 8:29), although the "pre" cannot be interpreted literally but only analogically, for if it were literally true, it would put God into before-and-after time.

I am grateful, not only for this profound theoretical and theological truth, but even more for its personal and practical impact on my faith and my life. It has guided me through the hardest darknesses and the severest sadnesses of my life. Significantly, Romans 8:29 (on predestination) comes immediately after Romans 8:28, which is my favorite verse in Scripture. I love the beginning of the Calvinist "Heidelberg Catechism": "What is your only comfort in life or in death?" "That both in life and in death I belong to my faithful Savior Jesus Christ."

I have called Romans 8:28 my "castle keep", my last and most impregnable defense against doubt and despair, because this incredibly good news—that "all things [without exception] work together for good [for those] who love God,... who are called according to his purpose"—logically and necessarily follows from the three most necessary and nonnegotiable attributes of God: His omnibenevolence, or unlimited goodness, which means goodwill, i.e., agape love; His omniscience, or unlimited wisdom and understanding; and His omnipotence, or unlimited and efficacious power. He wills only our best good; and He knows exactly what it is and how to get it; and He does get it, in the end; so that we can therefore thank Him for absolutely everything He brings into our lives, both the joys and the sufferings, and also everything He brings *out* of our lives by our free choices, except our sins—although even there He brings good out of evil, though only through the door of our (free) repentance: "where sin increased, grace abounded all the more" (Rom 5:20, KJV). If these three divine attributes are true; if God wants only our good and our joy, and if He infallibly knows what it is and how to get it; and if He has all the power over everything, even evil—well, then, we will necessarily get it—our very best good—in the end. His sovereignty, that is, the sovereignty of His love and wisdom, not just His power, guarantees it.

This is a precious truth that not only Calvinists but all Christians, and not only Christians but also Jews and Muslims, can believe, because it is guaranteed by the character of the God revealed in all three of those Abrahamic religions. No being deserves to be called "God" without these three attributes; a God cannot be wicked, stupid, or weak. Christians are more assured of this precious truth, of course, because they know Christ, not only as a great prophet who reveals God in his words and a great saint who reveals God in his character and life (which Jews and Muslims can also believe), but as God incarnate, God Himself, concretely, here in human time and human nature. God Himself died for us out of His crazy love for us.

Romans 8:28 is my answer to the problem of suffering and evil, which is both the most serious intellectual problem for a believer (if goodness is infinite, how can there be room for evil?) but also the most serious practical problem (how can I trust a God who allows in the life of all of us at least some of what He allowed in the life of Job?). God's total sovereignty is not merely proved deductively and theoretically by a syllogism (the one with those three nonnegotiable divine attributes as its three premises) but also proved inductively and practically by its success in doing something even better than removing sufferings: transforming them into goods, into aspects of God's goodwill and our joy. I think of the image of a great river flood that not only overcomes and smashes down all the dams in its way but also transforms the wood or concrete of the dams into parts of itself. The central and decisive example of this is of course Christ's Passion and death, the greatest evil and the greatest triumph of the Devil in history, which God used as the means to the greatest good in history, our salvation and our joy and glory.

I think of God's sovereignty as a circle with nothing outside it, rather like the universe itself. That is a good geometrical analogy for the theological point—as in Edwin Markham's poem "Outwitted":

"He drew a circle that shut me out—/Heretic, rebel, and thing to flout/But Love and I had the wit to win:/We drew a circle and took him in!"

"He" here is in fact Satan and his two sons, Sin (which is evil coming *from* us) and Suffering (which is evil coming *to* us), including even Death.

In fact, because of the principle in "Outwitted", one of the things that God's sovereignty includes and transforms is our free choices, both our choices to sin and our choices to repent. God's predestination is so complete that it includes our free will; so complete and all-inclusive that it even includes God's (ontological but not moral) permission to allow us to freely choose to sin. So ironically, what

Calvinism emphasizes (God's sovereignty over everything) entails the strongest justification for what Calvinism denies (free will). Calvinism's great truth refutes Calvinism's great falsehood.

There is nothing, absolutely nothing, that is outside the predestination, providence, and power of the God Who is infinite love and infinite wisdom and Whose whole will is for our greatest joy.

This teaching is not confined to Calvinism alone, of course, and the negative half of Calvin's version of it, his denial of human free will, is not only a heresy but also one with devastating possible consequences. For if we are not free, we are not morally responsible. For "ought" implies "can". But that logical consequence, by God's grace, almost no Calvinists, including Calvin himself, ever embrace. So Calvinists' logical "inconsistency" is their salvation from Calvinism's terrible logical "consistency".

For if we are not free, we are not morally responsible. And this is intolerable. In fact, if I had to do without either free will or without divine sovereignty, omnipotence, and predestination, I would without hesitation demand to keep free will. For even if God is only finitely good, wise, and powerful, He can still be loved and trusted somewhat, like a big brother; but if free will is gone, all moral meaning is gone. In fact, so is even the distinction between moral good and evil. And without that, all that would be left are the physical and emotional pleasures and pains common to both man and other higher animals.

Calvinism is a heresy. But every heresy is the perversion of a truth. It is usually one half of a difficult paradox without the other half— e.g., Christ's humanity without His divinity, or vice versa; or God's oneness without His Threeness, or vice versa. It is as important to keep and cherish the positive truth in a heresy as it is to avoid the negative error; it is as crucial to keep the true version as it is to reject the perversion.

᎒᎒ ᎒᎒ ᎒᎒

I am, of course, also grateful for the people closest to me and for what each has given me: my parents, my wife, my children, and my grandchildren and great-grandchildren. The joys have as vastly exceeded and overarched the sorrows and struggles and sufferings, as the stars in the sky have exceeded and overarched the worms in the earth.

I owe them all a great debt of gratitude. Please pray both for me and for them, dear reader: for John, Lucy, Maria, John, Jennifer, Katherine, Elizabeth, Rachel, Simon, Jake, Leo, Ashley, Kateri, Brendan, Rowan, and Stevie.

Now. Please. Literally.

Why? Because God is so astonishingly generous and merciful that even our pebble-sized prayers unleash avalanches of His grace.

30

Prospective

What Next?

Most certainly, most centrally, and most importantly, death.

Death is the greatest event in our lifetime because it is our passage into infinite life beyond time, forever. If we are "born again", it is our third birth.

What do I expect to happen at death? Everything the Church and her Scriptures tell me: the other three of the Four Last Things: Judgment, and Heaven or Hell, infinite, eternal, unimaginable joy or misery, fullness or emptiness.

Death is certain. It is not up to our choice. If the Satanically inspired geniuses in Silicon Valley ever complete the Promethean, Faustian, Baconian, distinctively modern project of "Man's conquest of Nature" by conquering Nature's trump card, death itself, by inventing artificial immortality by genetic or cybernetic engineering, my hope is that that will be the last generation of humanity because the fire from Heaven will mercifully descend and kill us all before an endless Hell on earth would ensue. As C. S. Lewis says, "We're like eggs at present. And you can't just go on being a 'good egg' forever; you must hatch or go bad."

Judgment is as certain as death. That is also not up to our choice. We may conquer death, but we cannot conquer judgment for we cannot conquer God and the divine, eternal, and necessary nature of truth and justice (which is simply moral truth).

And the either/or of Heaven or Hell is equally certain and not up to our choice. But which of those two it is, *is* our choice. As one Southern preacher not quite accurately but memorably put the dogma of free will, "God casts his vote for you and the Devil casts his vote against you and yours is the deciding vote." That is the ultimate foundation for all drama.

There is a Last Judgment because God is totally just and totally knowing. He is more than just, but not less. Truth is what He sees, not what we see. Our eternal fate depends on who we really are when we die, not who we think we are. Death punctures all sub-jectivist illusions, especially the ones preached by pop psychologists and commencement speakers. And we are responsible for who we are because who we are is above all what we have become by our choices. Because of God's justice, we all get what we most deeply want. And what we most deeply want (what Karl Rahner calls our "fundamental option") is what we will with our deepest heart: either "Thy will be done" or "My will be done." To put the same point in only apparently different words, God says to all of us, "Thy will be done", and only some of us return the favor and speak those same words back to Him. And those who say to God, "Thy will be done" *get* what God wills, which is our salvation and joy and glory; while others do not say that back to Him, and so they do *not* get what He wants, only what *they* want. So all get what they want: *not* God's will for them and therefore not joy, for that is His will for them. What could be more just? Eternal life is a gift, and a gift must be both freely given (which it always is, because the divine nature is unchangeable) and also freely accepted (which it *not* always is, because man is free).

I do not fear Hell, not because I am "good enough" for Heaven (no one is), but because God is "good enough". When God asks me why He should take me to Heaven, my answer will not begin with the word "I" but with the word "Thou".

But there are not just two but three possible immediate outcomes of the Last Judgment, or the "particular (individual) judgment", namely, immediate Hell, immediate Heaven, or immediate Purgatory and eventual Heaven. All in Purgatory are infallibly destined for Heaven. Purgatory is like Heaven's front porch, or Heaven's bathroom, where we go to get a hot shower to wash off all the stinky grime before we can participate in the great wedding feast. We will *want* those pains and embrace those pains, because in Purgatory we no longer sin and totally will God's will. That is why, despite Purgatory's pains, which exceed all earthly pains, its joys also exceed all earthly joys.

So why do I believe I will go to Purgatory before I go to Heaven? Why do I need the trip to the bathroom? The answer is obvious. Because I know what is in me, and the only place for some of it is the toilet. As I get older, I see more clearly my own faults, the gap between what I am now and what God insists I shall become. I see this more clearly now, not primarily because I see more clearly the Heavenly me that God insists I shall become, but because I see more clearly the earthly thing I now am. I see this especially when I compare my almost absentminded love for God and His children with that of the saints. (That is why saints make us uncomfortable and why the world resents them.)

The process of that Purgatorial change can be described in various ways: cleaning, de-rusting, strengthening, healing, maturing, getting fully baked instead of half-baked, learning, being sculpted, being molded, steel being fired, gold being purified, even toilet training. Justification was finished by Christ alone on the Cross, but sanctification is an ongoing process that requires our free cooperation. No one knows how long the Purgatorial process will take; Heavenly time measures earthly time, not vice versa.

C. S. Lewis, in his "golden sermon", "The Weight of Glory", says that if we saw the Heavenly, completed version of the dullest and most boring person we've ever met, we would be strongly tempted to fall down and worship him. Let that be premise #1. Let premise #2 be the fact that perhaps it is I who am the dullest person I've ever met. That is not far-fetched; in fact, there is evidence for it. For when I did Pascal's suggested experiment about "diversion" and did the surprisingly difficult thing of remaining in my own room with only myself as my companion for an hour without any distractions or diversions, I was more bored than I would have been if the most boring person I had ever met had been with me; does that not mean that I find myself the most boring person I've ever met? When I put these two premises together, I get the startling conclusion that if I saw my Heavenly self, I would be strongly tempted to worship him. The point of this syllogism is its corollary: that in order to transform me into *that*, God has to perform some very deep heart surgery in Purgatory's hospital.

And that is perhaps the most wonderful of all God's works. It is indeed wonderful that God the Father transformed Nothing into

Everything by the act of creation, by simply speaking His Word and sending His Spirit to blow on the formless waters of matter and create living beings. It is also wonderful that God the Son transformed water into wine at Cana, by invoking His Father and His Spirit. But it is even more wonderful that God will transform a sinner into a saint through His Son the Justifier and His Spirit the Sanctifier. For Nothingness put up no opposition to being transformed into Being by creation, and water did not talk back to Christ when He commanded it to become wine. In fact, in the words of the poet, when the Cana water saw its Lord, it "blushed". Nor did wine talk back when He transformed it into His Blood in the Last Supper and in the Eucharist. But sinners, by God's gift of free will, have a power that is not available to Nothingness or water or wine: the power to talk back, to argue, to resist God's will.

God uses everything, even our resistances, even our sins, as means to our salvation. There are no exceptions to the "all things" in Romans 8:28. Thus God used the sins of Joseph's brothers in selling Joseph into slavery to save them, as Joseph pronounced in the end: "You meant it for evil, but God meant it for good." Genesis 50:20 is one instance of Romans 8:28. Another, even greater one is the sins of those who crucified Christ—which is in fact every one of us. Like a judo master, God turns our very sinful efforts against themselves, if we repent and leap back into His mysterious river of Divine Providence. That wild and unpredictable river is the greatest of all dramas, "the greatest story ever told". As Saint Thérèse of Lisieux said, "*Everything* is a grace." The sister of Harry Jellema, my favorite teacher, told me that those were Dr. Jellema's dying words. His final philosophy lecture.

One precious Catholic truth that I learned as an Evangelical (and this is the essential reason Evangelicals are so often full of joy) is that my salvation does not depend on my holiness but on God's love. I can refuse salvation, but I cannot merit it; I can undo it, but I cannot do it. He does it. My only hope, my only plea, is Jesus Christ; it is not me.

The reason I do not fear Hell is Him, not me. I find Saint Faustina's simple prayer "Jesus, I trust in You" immensely freeing because it means that I do not have to trust in myself. At one point in his struggles, Job was so foolish as to say: "I take my stand on my integrity" (JB translation). That reminds me of a line from Ed Muskie, the Maine Democrat who many years ago was a candidate for the Democratic Presidential primary and was campaigning in Iowa to a large field of Republican farmers. They had forgotten to bring a stage or platform, so nobody but the front row could see him. He spotted a large piece of farm equipment, asked what it was, and was told that it was a manure spreader, so he climbed up on it to speak, and began, "This is the first time in my life I have given a Democratic speech from a Republican platform." I hope that when Luther, facing his heresy trial, said his famous words, "Here I stand, I cannot do otherwise, God help me", he was thinking of Christ, not himself, as his platform to stand on.

I expect great joy in Purgatory, as well as great pain. I think it will feel like a snake being stripped of its old, ugly, dead skin, or like a Band-Aid over my whole body (and soul!) being torn off. Whether the Band-Aid comes off all at once (which is, I think, a *theologoumenon*, or possible opinion, that Purgatory is instantaneous) or gradually (which is more likely, and the majority opinion) does not change the *amount* of pain, only the timing of it.

Purgatory is decreed by God's love. Love multiplies both joy and sorrow by the number of people loved and by the depth of that love. God's love for us is unlimited, and therefore so is His sorrow for our sins. I think that when we feel the strange juxtaposition of great sorrow and great joy in Him, whether now or in Heaven, we will feel also that same strange juxtaposition in our response to it.

And that juxtaposition of joy and sorrow is the Christian solution to suffering not just in Purgatory but in this life, too: our sufferings become salvific when we "offer them up" in union with Christ and His sufferings. For that union is not merely *imitation* but *incorporation*. Corrie ten Boom, asked why she was so sure she could never slip between Jesus' fingers, replied, "Because I am one of His fingers." Because we are "in" Him and He is "in" us, our sufferings can also be His and His can be ours. And that means that they can also be joys precisely *because* they are in Him and because He is in them. "In-ness" is the source of all joy because it is the very nature of the Trinity.

And in Purgatory we will know that, and see that, and feel that, and therefore we will *want*, we will passionately long for, our sufferings because we will see Him in them, as the greatest of saints do already on earth. I am as far from that as New York is far from San Francisco. But it is in the same country, and that country has many roads to walk on. The roads all have bumps in them, but the roads are bigger than the bumps.

One More Prediction about Purgatory

Here is one more reason for my expectation of joy in Purgatory.

A few days ago I picked up one of the books I wrote, which was published many years ago. I had forgotten about it, and I was surprised to be surprised about it: both about what I had written, since I had forgotten it, and about how good I could not help honestly thinking it was. "Wow. That's a really good idea. I wonder who thought of that? Good grief, it was me." It was like reaching for a friend's hand in a darkened room and finding your own where you expected to find his: "What am *I* doing *out there*?"

Then two thoughts immediately came to me: first, that authors are often the last people in the world who can be expected to have a fair and accurate judgment about the worth of their works, and secondly, that pride and self-centeredness are at the center and foundation of Original Sin.

Then I thought that there might be a profound Christian truth hidden in the pagan myth about the river Lethe, which, in Greek mythology, we must cross when we die. *Lethe* means "forgetting", and when we cross that river we forget our past earthly life. I do not think that is literally true, because memory is a good thing, and no good thing is simply and totally lost in the afterlife, but only transformed. But what if the transformation consisted of forgetting, not one single thing that we did or made or accomplished, but only our own ownership of these things? What if I could read all the books I have written (which now number over one hundred) without the two fears I had when I remembered that I had written that good idea? Nothing but the ego would be subtracted. All the ego's good and true and beautiful objects would remain, and be cleansed of the double trouble of egotism, intellectual inaccuracy and prejudice and moral pride and possessiveness? It would be like discovering a friend you could admire and trust and enjoy as a true "soul-mate".

Imagine Aquinas discovering that someone else had written the *Summa*. How much more would he enjoy it! Imagine Tolkien discovering *The Lord of the Rings* and *The Silmarillion*. Imagine the builders of the great cathedrals entering one of those almost-supernatural masterpieces as a wide-eyed peasant. (They almost had that joy in this life, for these greatest works of art on earth were almost always designed and built anonymously!) C. S. Lewis said that he wrote the books he wished someone else would write, but they didn't, so he had to. That's a second best. Unplanned discovery is more joyful than planned for the same reason that loving others brings us more joy than loving ourselves.

In Heaven we will wear crowns, and we will throw them and their jewels (our virtues and achievements) at the feet of Christ and say, "They are Yours." And He will take His crown, with its thorns, and say, "And this is yours." So the difference between Heaven (that first thing) and Purgatory (that second thing) may disappear!

This subtraction of the ego from all our achievements would be both Purgatory—a subtraction, a loss, a suffering—and Heaven—an addition, a plus, a joy. Saint Catherine said there would be great joys as well as sufferings in Purgatory, so this will likely be one of those joys. And C. S. Lewis said that there may be great pains in Heaven, and if so we would desire them deeply and find them blessed. Perhaps this is one of them.

We are commanded to love our neighbors as ourselves. (Note bene, we are commanded, not recommended; and God will not rest until we have learned to obey His commandments perfectly.) Logically, that necessarily means that we must also love ourselves. Perhaps this is how we will accomplish that: by seeing our own accomplishments as the accomplishments of someone else, by the Heavenly "forgetfulness" above. Thus I would love another as myself by loving myself as another. We would not forget anything good in our life, only the ego that claimed it.

And this could cover absolutely everything in our lives. We would see our life as God sees it, not only accurately but also lovingly. Truth and love, after all, are the two highest values in life. And if we share the divine nature (2 Pet 1:4, KJV), we would love as God loves even when we loved ourselves: unselfishly.

Accurately and wisely, therefore seeing how all the sufferings, and even all the sins, which God allowed us to commit, were redeemed (though only through our repentance and His atonement) and incorporated into the greater good and the greater joy. Perhaps we would forget the ownership of our sins as well as of our virtues and accomplishments, and thus see both truly.

The practical difference this speculation about the afterlife makes to this life is immense. To practice this forgetfulness before death could become one of life's greatest joys. When you do a good deed of charity, Christ says, "Let not your right hand know what your left hand does." Why carry around that dead carcass of the albatross that He has already put to death on the Cross? Why claim ownership of your very life, of your very self, if instead you can say "Not I, but Christ lives in me"? The absence of the ego is as necessary a part of the "package deal" and its joy as is the presence of Christ. The "not I" looks like the letter "I" crossed out: it looks like a cross. It is the only real alchemy: it turns wood to gold.

A Last Word

I claim, as the life preserver that I will never let go, Christ's promise "Lo, I am with you always, even unto the end of the world" (Mt 28:20, KJV). The RSV has "behold" instead of "lo", but faith is more like a hearing than a beholding, more like an ear than an eye. In the darkness of the storm, faith hears His words, "It is I, be not afraid" (Mt 14:27, KJV). As with the Eucharist, so with life: "Sight, taste, and touch are all deceived; the ear alone most safely is believed. I believe all the Son of God has spoken; than Truth's own word there is no truer token" (Saint Thomas Aquinas).

"Truth's own word" is love. "God *is* love." Kierkegaard wrote, somewhere, that even if everything he ever wrote was false, one thing must necessarily be true: "that God is love". Not just for Himself, but also for us. For me. For you. Personally, individually, with terrible concreteness.

If you know that, you are happy, even if you do not feel happy. If you do not know that, you are unhappy, even if you do not feel unhappy. It is astonishing how easily we identify our own feelings with the infallible criterion of truth! Faith is not a feeling, and neither is love. If you believe in that divine love and trust that love, then nothing is lacking, no matter what else you lack. If you do not believe it and trust it, then everything is lacking, no matter what else you have. Saint Augustine says, "He who has God, has everything, even if he has nothing else; and he who does not have God has nothing, even if he has everything else; and he who has both God and everything else has no more than he who has God only." If that is not true, then God is not God, but just *a* god.

Gratefully to plagiarize Cardinal Sarah's title, it's "God or nothing".

As a philosopher and an admirer of Socrates, I think it fitting for me to end with a question: So which of the two do you choose?